You *Can* Quilt It!

You *Can* Quilt It!

Stunning Free-Motion Quilting Designs Made Easy

Deborah M. Poole

Dedication

To my husband, Jace, who goaded me into learning how to run my long-arm quilting machine by saying, "You know what I think? You're afraid of that machine."

You *Can* Quilt It!
Stunning Free-Motion Quilting Designs Made Easy

Martingale®
19021 120th Ave. NE, Ste. 102
Bothell, WA 98011-9511 USA
ShopMartingale.com

Printed in China
19 18 17 16 15 14 8 7 6 5 4 3 2 1

Library of Congress Cataloging-in-Publication Data is available upon request.

ISBN: 978-1-60468-295-3

Mission Statement

Dedicated to providing quality products and service to inspire creativity.

Credits

PRESIDENT AND CEO: Tom Wierzbicki
EDITOR IN CHIEF: Mary V. Green
DESIGN DIRECTOR: Paula Schlosser
MANAGING EDITOR: Karen Costello Soltys
ACQUISITIONS EDITOR: Karen M. Burns
TECHNICAL EDITOR: Ellen Pahl
COPY EDITOR: Marcy Heffernan
PRODUCTION MANAGER: Regina Girard
COVER AND INTERIOR DESIGNER: Adrienne Smitke
PHOTOGRAPHER: Brent Kane
ILLUSTRATOR: Rose Wright

Contents

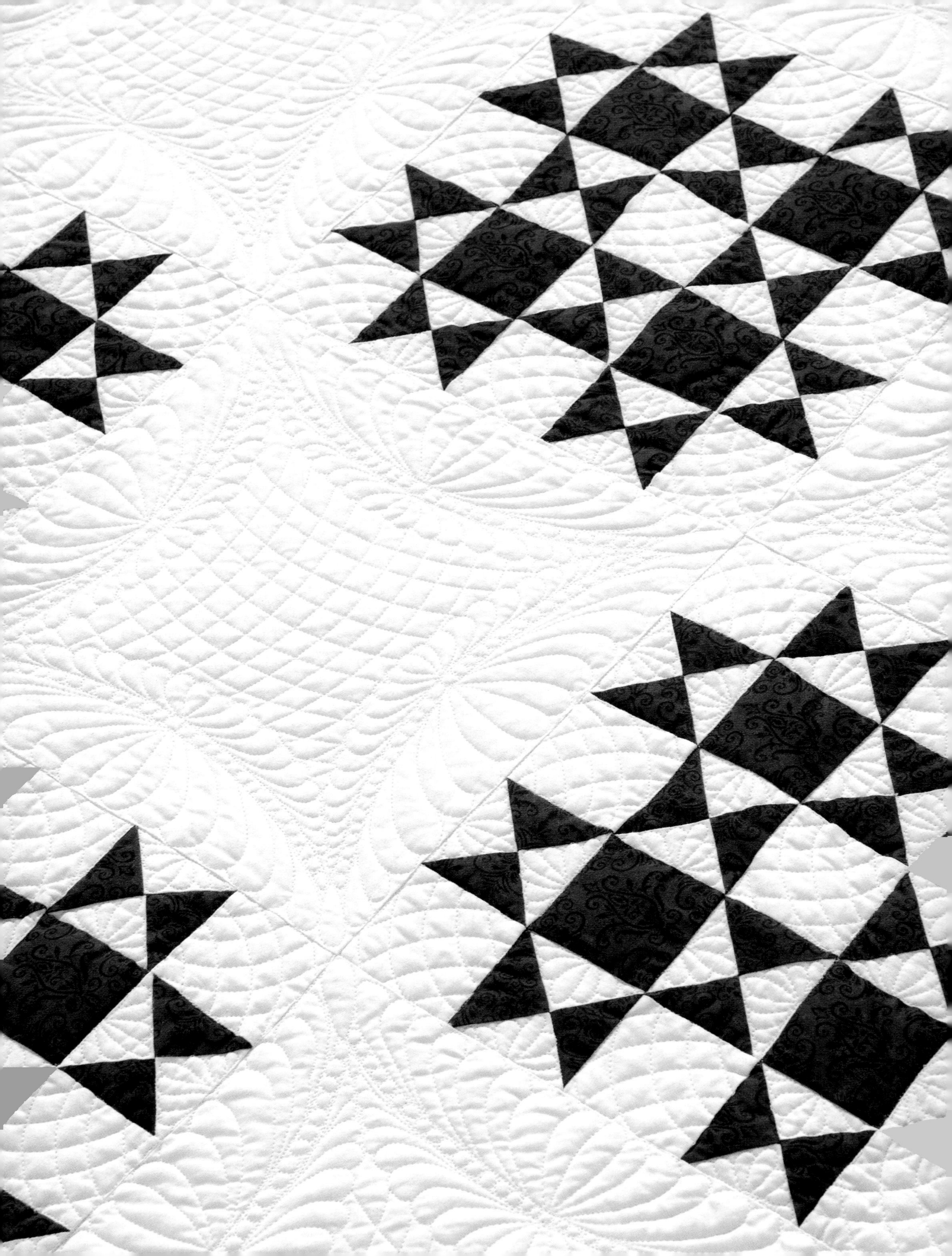

Introduction

Have you ever gone to a quilt show or quilt shop, or looked through quilting books and, admiring all the beautiful machine quilting designs, asked yourself, "How did she do that? How did she get her quilting so perfect?" Then, in that same moment thought, "Oh, I could never do that!"

Well I'm here to tell you, *yes*, you *can* quilt it!

For years I was a dyed-in-the-wool hand quilter. I didn't think it was a quilt unless it was made entirely by hand—including all the patchwork. Slowly I crossed over to the dark side and started piecing with a sewing machine. However, machine quilting was where I drew the line. I was not *ever* going to quilt by machine. It would still be a quilt if quilted by hand.

Unfortunately, as my resolve deepened to hand quilt only, my stack of unfinished tops also deepened. It was getting pretty dark on my side of the line I'd drawn. But wait! Was that light I saw? Light on the other side of the line? Finally, after being buried in quilt tops, I once again crossed over to the other side and purchased my long-arm machine.

At first I too asked the questions, *How did she quilt that? How did she get her quilting so perfect?* and thought, *Oh, I could never do that!* Worse, I was unable to find books to answer the most important questions I had. Through perseverance, study, and just out-and-out hair pulling, I've finally achieved my style of quilting. That style? Making hand-guided machine quilting look as though it were achieved by a computer.

With this book, you'll have a shortcut—I'm giving you in a matter of pages what took me several years to discover. I reveal many of the little secrets you've been wondering about, and answer questions you've been asking but could never find the answers to. Most importantly, this book will take you from feeling like you could never attain such a high level of quilting to a *YES, I* can *quilt it!* attitude.

How to Use This Book

If you're like me, you'll want to skip right to the "good stuff." However, I suggest you read the beginning sections first. I've written this book with the viewpoint that you, the reader, have some machine-quilting experience and aren't a first timer. Meaning, I won't cover things such as batting, thread, needles, loading the quilt, or tension issues. There are many good books out there that already cover those things. My desire is to give you the answers to questions I had when first learning, such as, "Do I have to mark the quilt? Do I have to backtrack, or do I stop and start *a lot*?" And most importantly, "How do I stitch out that design?"

While this book is written from a long-arm quilter's perspective, many of the techniques and most of the designs are also appropriate for those who quilt on a domestic home sewing machine.

Studying the first few sections will familiarize you with the tools and techniques needed to achieve the good stuff. These first sections will give you many dos and a few don'ts. If you're a feather nut like myself, you'll especially want to look at my section on feathers. I'm often told I make the most beautiful feathers this or that person has ever seen. My feather section will help you achieve the same type of feathers I use in every quilt I stitch.

Lastly, I'd like you to keep in mind that all of my practices and prejudices are just that—mine. There's no one correct way to achieve anything. Just because I instruct one way in this book, while you or someone you know does it differently, it doesn't mean you're wrong or I'm right. It just means we arrived by different paths. I treat my quilting just like I do my driving. My husband says, "I don't think there's a road you haven't driven down." I like to take different roads to get to old destinations, and there certainly is never one pathway to quilting. I believe I can never stop learning different ways to quilt. Trying new ways makes the journey more interesting.

Using Templates and Rulers

In this section, I'll cover the tools I use for my success. Please remember these are the things I personally use. You may find one that works better for you. These suggestions are intended to give you a jumping-off point.

I don't stitch any top without reaching for a template or ruler of some sort. These tools are ¼"-thick acrylic templates that long-arm and mid-arm machine quilters use to guide their hopping foot and create different shapes.

The hopping foot on a long-arm machine is a ½"-diameter circular foot that literally hops up and down. It looks like the darning foot used on home sewing machines for free-motion quilting, but it acts more like a walking foot. However, unlike the walking foot, it allows you to do everything in free motion.

Keep in mind that templates and rulers are not the finished size. Your hopping foot adds ¼" to ½", depending on the brand of your machine.

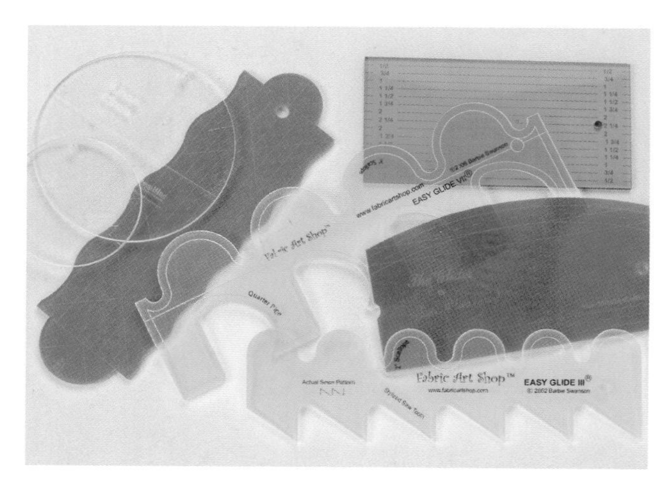

A selection of quilting templates and rulers

An extended base plate for the throat of your long-arm machine is a must-have. These base plates support the templates as you sew on your long-arm or mid-arm machine. Without one, your templates will teeter and can slip between your needle and your hopping foot. If your machine didn't come equipped with one, you'll need to purchase one. Contact your dealer. Or do an online search for "extended base plate [insert your machine name here]." I use the one that came with my machine, but there are after-market plates as well.

Extended base plate for long-arm machine

STRAIGHT-EDGE RULERS

I have several straight-edge rulers I like. A short 2" x 4" ruler is great for sashing work and stitching in the ditch around both patchwork and appliqué. I also keep close at hand a 2" x 12" ruler marked at ¼" intervals.

CIRCLE AND OVAL TEMPLATES

I've spent literally hundreds, even thousands of dollars on ¼"-thick acrylic templates I've never used. When presented with the frequent question, "Which templates should I purchase?" I want to be perfectly honest. This is a difficult question to answer because everyone's style of quilting is different. An art quilter, for instance, rarely, if ever, uses templates, and if you aspire to be an art quilter, purchasing certain templates would be a waste of your money.

Circle templates are so versatile. I use them for designs ranging from feathered wreaths, to egg and dart, to continuous curve, to curved crosshatching, and the list goes on and on. In my quilting, it's rare that I don't use at least one circle template on a quilt.

So, for the style of quilting found throughout this book, if you can afford it, purchase every size of circle template available. When I started out, I purchased only the even sizes. I learned to make do, which is probably a good thing, because a lot of what I learned from making do, I'll teach you here. But, if you don't want to struggle, do extra math, and pull out a lot of your hair, purchase those extra sizes. On my award-winning quilt "Dresden's Dilemma," shown above right, I used virtually every size circle from a 4" to a 12" (the largest made), and I had to fudge it for sizes up to 15".

"Dresden's Dilemma"

If you can't afford every size, I suggest you purchase templates in ½" increments. I know, you're probably thinking, "What? Most quilt blocks and sashings finish in a whole-number size, not a half size." Remember, the long-arm foot is ½" in diameter, adding ¼" to any straight-edge template and ½" to any template that is closed, such as a circle, flower, or heart. This means when you sew around a 4"-circle template, the foot adds ½" to your stitched circle; thus your circle will be 4½", not 4". If you want to stitch a finished 4" circle, you need to start with a 3½"-circle template.

Oval templates are not an up-front must-have, but they offer longer-edged options for stitching curved crosshatching, continuous curves, and long egg-and-dart patterns in sashings. I suggest you get a set at some point.

TIME TO PRACTICE

Using templates and rulers takes a good amount of practice, but once you become confident, quilting with them is as easy as quilting without them. I suggest that you load a practice quilt sandwich and do just that—practice. It won't matter if your circles have a flat side or your straight edges have a wobble (or six). Get acquainted with your templates and rulers.

Key Point~Lighten Up

Templates don't have wings, so don't press on them as if they're trying to take flight. Everyone's first reaction to using templates is, the harder I press, the better they'll stay in place. Not true. Give your shoulder, back, and arm muscles a break; the templates really aren't going anywhere. They may slide a little, but that's what the practice is for—learning the right amount of pressure to apply for each shape and size. And believe me, it's different for each.

If you find yourself tensing up, just walk away, shake it off, read a book, or watch a TV show. The tenser you are, the harder you'll push down on the template. I don't think I need to tell you how I know this—as I said before, it happens to everyone.

You'll need to learn to use both hands when working with templates and rulers, so change it up. When working with straight edges, practice stitching in all directions. Make angles, work toward yourself and away from yourself, first with your right hand guiding the machine, and your left holding the ruler, and then switch. Remember that the hopping foot will add ¼" along the edges of straight rulers. When placing your ruler for designs such as crosshatching, place it ¼" from where you actually want to stitch. As you practice, the spacing will become automatic.

Straight ruler used to guide hopping foot

STITCHING CIRCLES

Unless you're a magician, there's no way to make circles without switching hands on your template. Even someone as experienced as me can only make it halfway to three-quarters of the way around a circle template before having to switch hands and reposition. For this reason, I prefer solid circle templates versus nesting circles. A solid circle is stabler—you can get your whole hand on the surface to hold it in place as you stitch around it. With a nesting circle, you can only steady it with a couple of fingers, and you can only stitch around larger circles a portion of a side at a time. When making a complete circle, I always start at the top and proceed clockwise.

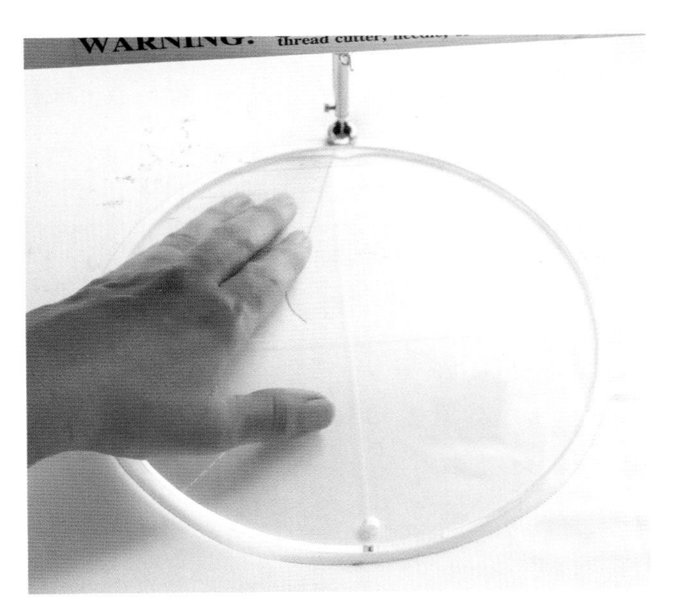

Begin at the top of a circle.

Stitch as far as you can, stop with the needle in the down position, carefully reposition your hands, and continue stitching to close the circle. If you need to stop and reposition several times, that's fine too. Do whatever suits you best.

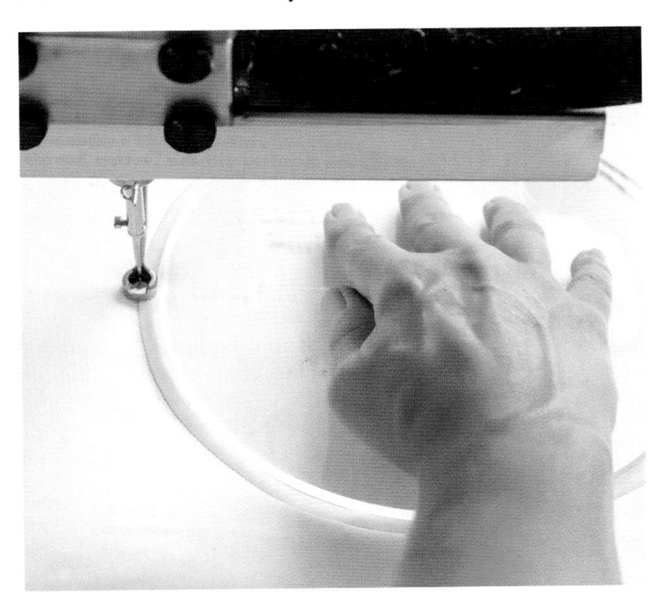

Work clockwise around the circle template.

Key Point~Practice, Practice, Practice

I'm sure most of us have heard about PPPing. It stands for Practice, Practice, Practice. PPPing for me means, "Perfect Practice Makes Perfect Performance." My first tip is to slow down. Muscle memory is important, but if you practice incorrectly your muscles remember the incorrect motions, and you have to retrain. If you think you're already going slowly, go even slower. It will seem tedious at first, but slowing down will save you lots of ripping in the end.

MISCELLANEOUS TEMPLATES AND RULERS

The first template/ruler I purchased is the only one I'll mention by name, since there is no other like it: the VersaTool by Handi Quilter. This little ruler lives up to its name, being very versatile. While small, it's a great aid in making short straight edges, quilting continuous curves, stitching in the ditch, and for creating egg-and-dart patterns.

I also use a large wedge-shaped template called a Baptist Fan template for larger circles and curved crosshatching.

Hit the Mark—Stencils, Pencils, and More

When I was first getting started in machine quilting, I had so many questions about marking the quilt top. I've experimented and learned a lot since then and will share that information with you in this section to help you get a head start.

STENCILS

Intricately cut stencils are a great tool, and they're actually fairly inexpensive. I used them extensively when I first started out. Now, however, I use very few premade stencils and often make my own. Any plastic template material found at your local quilt shop will work. I mainly use this product to mark registration lines, which you'll learn about in the next section.

Another of my must-haves is a drafting or architectural circle template for drawing very small circles. These templates are available in art-supply stores. Try not to let your quilting thoughts be ruled by quilting products only, especially when making stencils. I've been known to use dishes, cans from the pantry cupboard, cardboard, and even pipe cleaners when trying to achieve the shape I desire.

Assorted stencils for marking designs on quilt tops

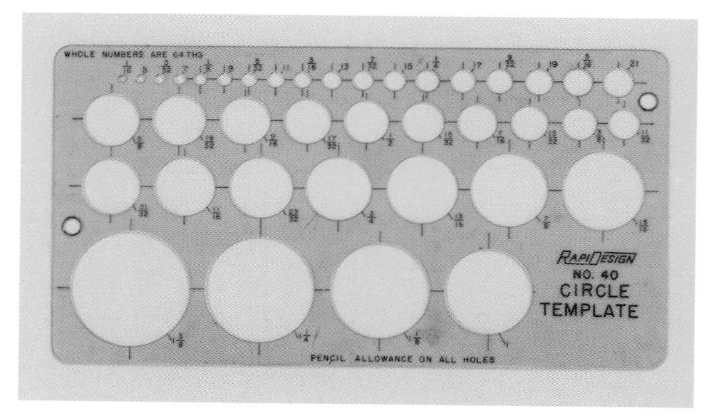

Drafting template with range of circle sizes

MARKING TOOLS

Marking tools are another area where I've spent much time, effort, and money to find what suits me best. That's not to say there aren't plenty of other good products out there; these are just my personal preferences. The best thing to do is try several types and find your own personal favorite. However, my list (right) will be a good starting point.

Assorted marking tools

Key Point~Test Mark First

Be sure to pretest any product on a swatch of the fabric you're going to mark before using it on the whole quilt. Though it happens very rarely, a marking tool and fabric combination can bond with each other, and the marks could become permanent.

I mark most of my quilts while they're on the frame. I like this method because I want my markings very light so they're easily removed, especially on client quilts. If you premark, there's the chance of lighter markings rubbing off in the loading and rolling process. Occasionally I mark before loading, but only if the spacing is very precise and needs to be exact.

Chaco Liner. When marking a quilt on the frame, I use Clover's Chaco Liner on medium to dark fabrics. This product is a chalk roller that goes on very fine and is very maneuverable. The marks are trouble-free to remove, the roller is easy to refill, and it's found in most fabric stores. The markings also show up on many cream or tan fabrics.

Pounce pad. I also use the pounce pad, but use it strictly with stencils. For a more even, lighter, and easier application, rather than using the included pad, I use a foam paintbrush found at any home-improvement or craft store. Removing the markings is simple; just follow the included instructions.

Fine-line marking pen. For any fabrics too light for the Chaco Liner, I use the fine-line blue water-erasable marking pen by Collins. I like this pen because it has a very fine line, and with just a spritz of water the blue line easily disappears. While I've never had an issue with this pen, I do recommend using it only if you plan on fully submerging your finished quilt in water to remove any residues from the pen.

Mechanical chalk pencil. I also use a mechanical chalk pencil. There are several brands, but I exclusively use the Bohin pencil. Again, this pencil marks with a very fine line, and if you mark light enough, in most cases the stitching causes the drawn line to disappear. When the stitching doesn't cover the marks, they disappear effortlessly with the included eraser.

Key Point~Test Colored Pencils

Chalk pencils come in several colors. I've only used the white chalk. If you use one of the colored chalks, be sure to pretest thoroughly on a swatch of fabric.

Registration Lines—The Key to Perfection

Registration lines may not be the key to perfection, but they're certainly the key to the *illusion* of perfection!

Being a rigid personality type and having a background steeped in hand quilting, I soon became very frustrated with inaccuracy when I first started machine quilting. My feathered wreaths weren't exactly round or even close to round, and my serpentine feathers in a border were more fat than thin or vice versa. While looking at other machine-quilted quilts, I observed this indeed was the case for most machine quilters. I wasn't the only one. Many feathered wreaths, including my own, looked much like the drawing below.

Certainly not horrible; however, referring back to my rigid personality, I knew this would not be good enough for me. I needed to find a way to make my feathered wreaths as round as if I had hand quilted them using a stencil, but without marking each feather as you do with hand quilting. The answer was really quite simple—registration lines.

I actually mark very little on my quilt tops. I don't mark each individual feather or tiny circle. What I do mark are registration lines and hash marks to use as guides. Let's look at a feathered wreath as an example. The registration lines for this wreath will be two concentric circles.

Feathered wreath

Compare the circles and you'll see that the registration lines are the *finished edges* of the wreath, not a guide for the stem. I'll use a circle template to stitch the stem, also known as a spine. By marking the finished interior and exterior edges, I can stitch perfectly round wreaths every time.

Let's look at the registration lines for my Feathered Four block as an example. This design consists of feathers stitched around four pumpkin seed shapes in the center. The finished block and the corresponding registration lines are both shown at right.

Notice there are three different levels of hash marks and registration lines, labeled A, B, and C. The real purpose of these lines is to create uniformity—the illusion of perfection. It doesn't really matter if the teardrops on the inner and outer levels are the same size or shape just so long as they all start roughly the same distance from the corner. The inner hash marks (A) show you where to stop and start your pumpkin seed, again the illusion of perfection. The "true" registration line (B), the wall your feather will bump up against, adds to this illusion, as does the stem-line marking (C).

As long as at least two elements of your design are uniform, the overall design will give the illusion of perfection. In the Feathered Four design, if your pumpkin seeds and stem lines appear to be uniform and equal, this design will look computer generated.

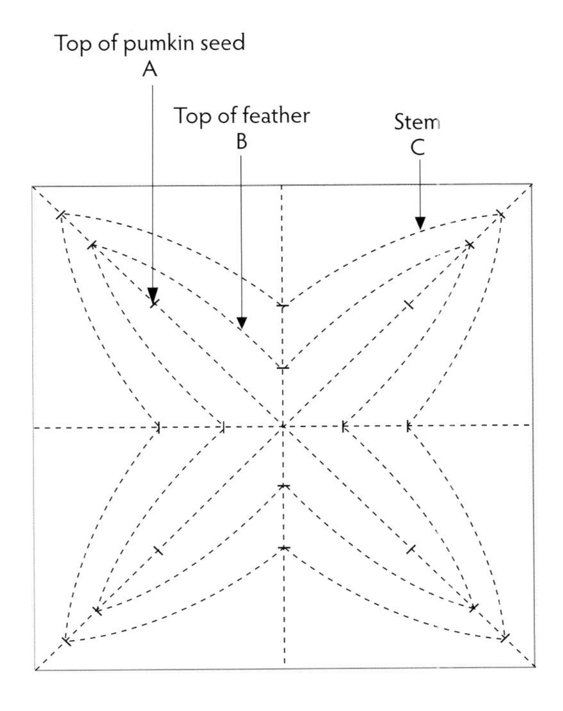

Feathered four

Feathered Friends

Big feathers, little feathers, feathers that curve and bend. Feathers—I *love* feathers, they make a quilt dance and sing. Many new and even experienced machine quilters have what I call feather-phobia. For some reason they think they can't even *try* to make feathers. Feathers are not just for the expert. I promise that feathers, with some PPPing, are as easy as making loops.

When I first started long-arm machine quilting, I took a sketch pad and pencil everywhere I went, and in any spare moment I practiced drawing feathers. I hate to admit it, but that sketch pad and pencil even went to church with me and were used while I listened to the sermon. I made stems of every shape and size, and feathered them. By doing this, I discovered what type of feathers I liked, and what type I didn't.

Feathers come in all shapes and sizes. Short and chunky, long and skinny, they can be shaped like a traditional feather, like a paisley, a leaf, or even a flame. The options are boundless. For the purposes of this book I'll focus on the traditional paisley-shaped feather.

I use three different styles of feather, depending on the formality of the quilt.

The long-arm feather. The long-arm feather is the first type of feather created on a long-arm machine. It is great for informal quilts. The individual feathers are less uniform and open; they give a quilt a folksy feel. This is an ideal feather for a beginner.

Long-arm feathers

The lace feather. This feather adds a lacey look and feel to a quilt. It has the wow factor without being difficult to execute. A series of these feathers can turn a ho-hum quilt into something stunning. I sometimes call it a *non-backtrack feather,* because there is no backtracking (stitching over previously stitched lines). It, too, is a great feather for a beginner.

Lace or non-backtrack feathers

The heirloom feather. The heirloom feather is the most formal and also the most difficult to execute. It's my personal favorite, and it's used for most of the illustrations in this book. Heirloom feathers are best used when you want the quilting, rather than the patchwork, to shine. Used in large open spaces and borders, this feather makes a quilt a showstopper.

Heirloom feathers

ANATOMY OF A FEATHER

Feathers have several different elements. Let's review their parts.

Feather. Each individual paisley shape is one feather.

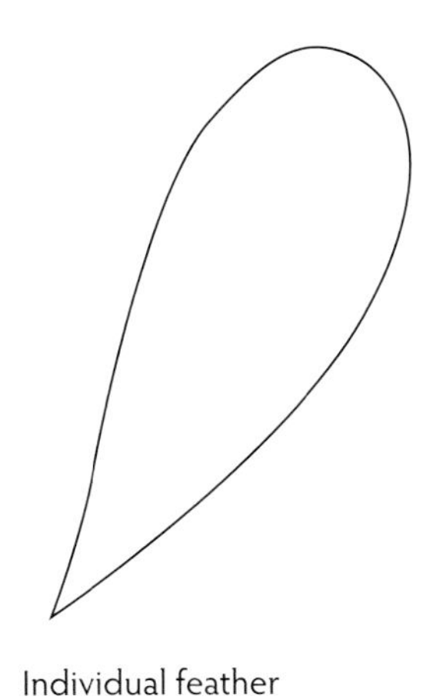

Individual feather

Plume or frond. The plume, or frond, is the collection of feathers forming a uniform shape. In the example shown, three plumes create a motif.

Three plumes

Stem/shaft/vein/spine. These terms are all interchangeable. The stem is the spine, so to speak, of the plume. You attach the individual feathers to the stem.

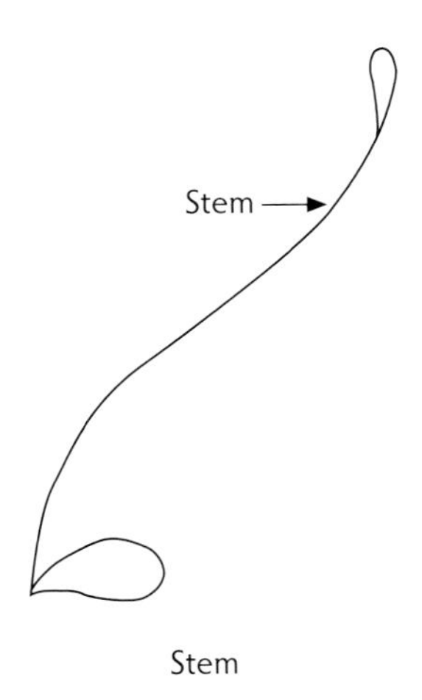

Stem

Quill and cap. The quill is the bottom end of the feather that attaches to the stem. The shape of the quill determines the elegance of the overall motif. The cap is simply the top part of the feather, opposite the quill.

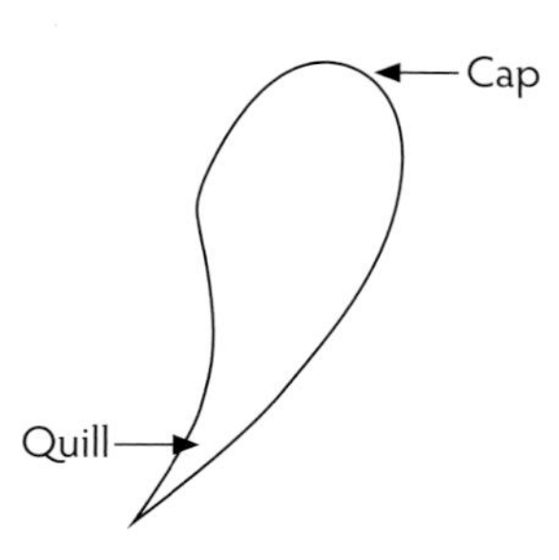

QUILLS AND FEATHER ELEGANCE

When you think of a feather, think of a paisley, half of a heart, or a teardrop. These are all good shapes for feather making. Study the three variations in the illustration below, and then we'll apply those shapes to some stems.

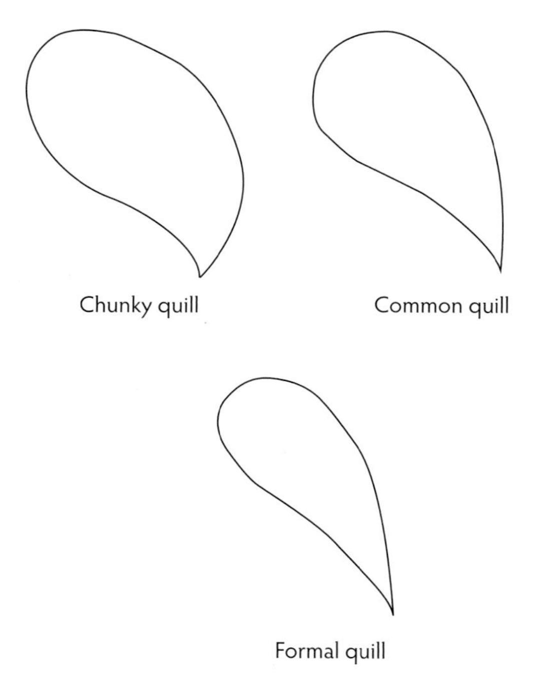

Note how the chunky feathers are playful. I like to use feathers like these on baby quilts or brightly colored quilts.

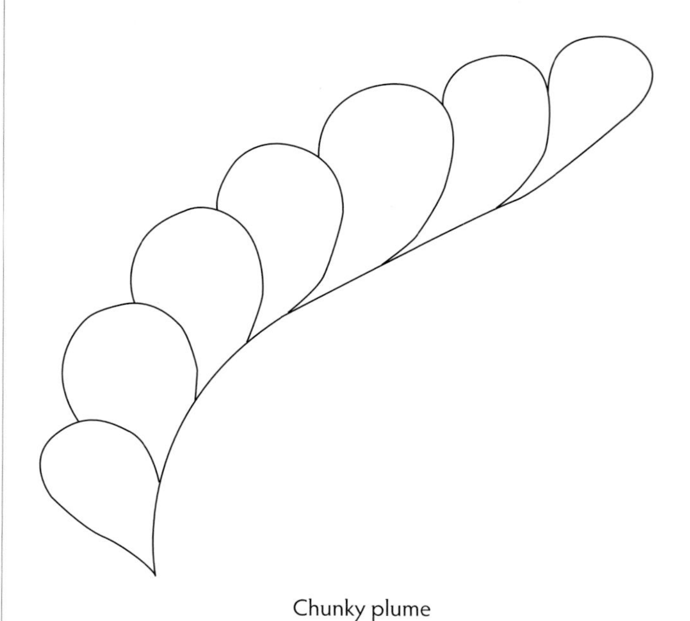

Chunky plume

The common quill feathers are probably the most familiar—not too playful, and not too formal. These feathers are appropriate on any quilt.

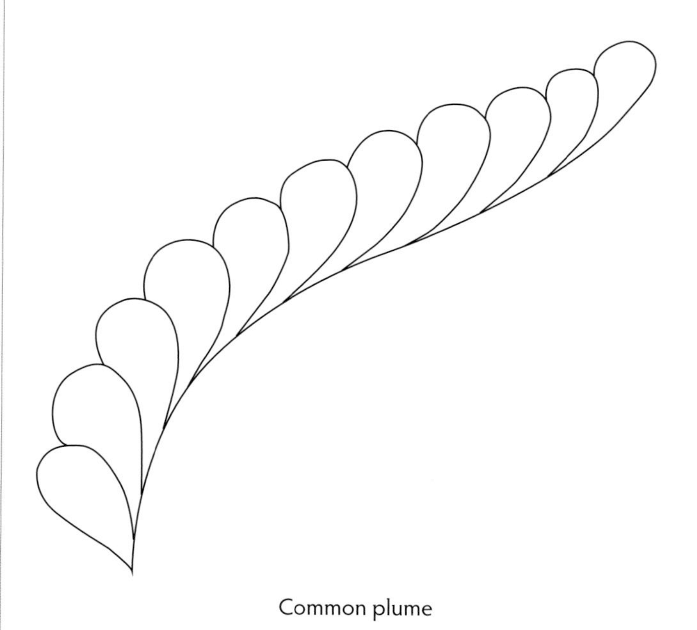

Common plume

Formal quill feathers are what I refer to as heirloom or Victorian feathers and are best saved for the most formal of quilts. Note how the longer quill gives the feather the illusion of waving or curling away from the stem.

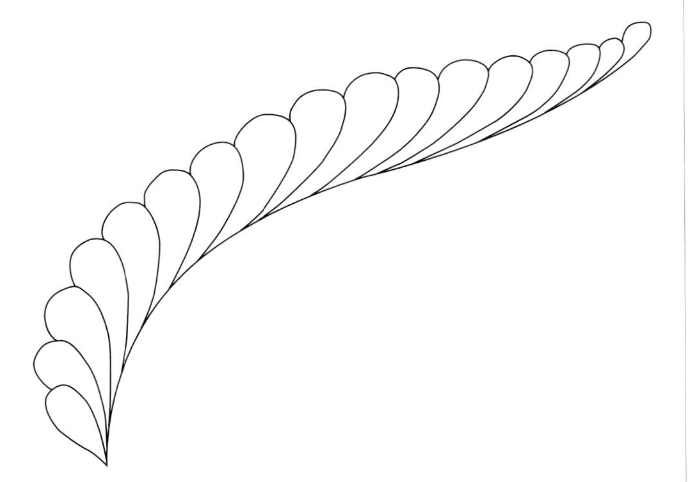

Formal plume

STEMS AND FEATHER ELEGANCE

Now let's talk about stem shape. Sometimes, especially in narrow borders and sashing, you have no other choice—the stem must be straight. Typically, I like to add curves if at all possible. The more curve you can add to your stem, the more interesting it becomes.

If you're trying to fill a border with feathers, a straight-line stem will work just fine.

Straight stem used in border

Adding curves, however, makes the entire motif more graceful and elegant.

Curved stem used in border

When making your feathers, you want the tops or caps of each to be rounded like a balloon. Also make sure the feather cap curls all the way to the top of the adjacent feather so it appears to be behind the preceding feather, the one you just stitched.

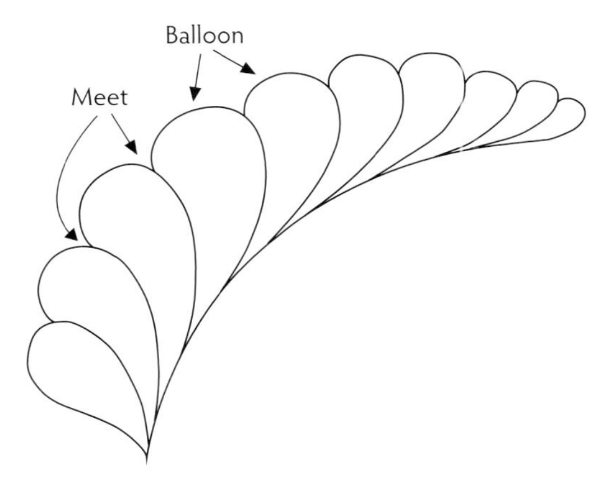

Many beginners tend to flatten out the top of the feather. Don't fall into that trap. Remember, perfect practice makes perfect performance. So slow down and concentrate on making round tops every time. Remember the balloon.

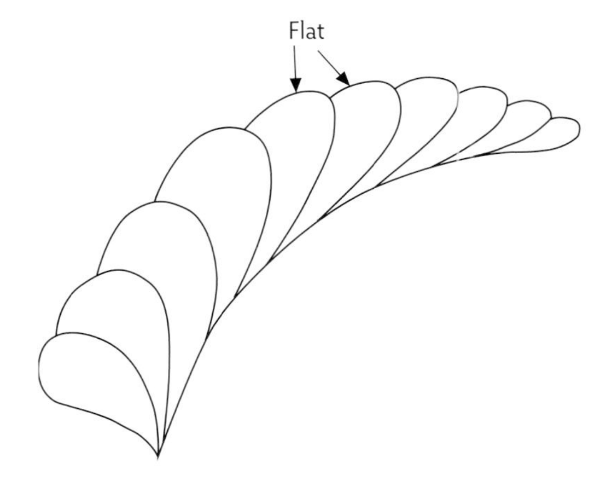

CURVING FEATHERS

Stitching feathers on an inside curve can be tricky. You want to avoid the "long finger" look if possible. Don't worry if it happens, occasionally I still get trapped by it. Just move on and correct it on the next curve.

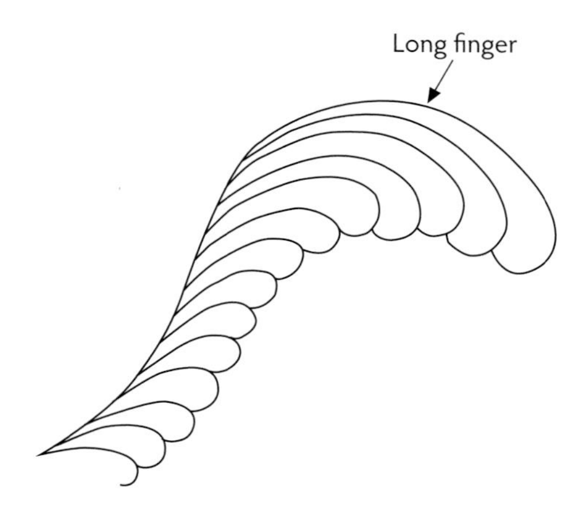

The simplest way to avoid the dreaded finger is to widen the quills.

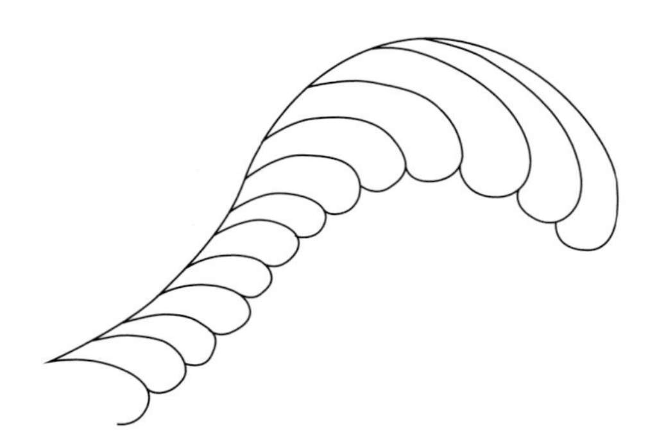

However, the wider quill takes away from the elegance of the feather. Another way to deal with this situation is to add a teardrop and build off of it. A teardrop is usually the first feather in a plume and is smaller and less paisley-shaped than other feathers.

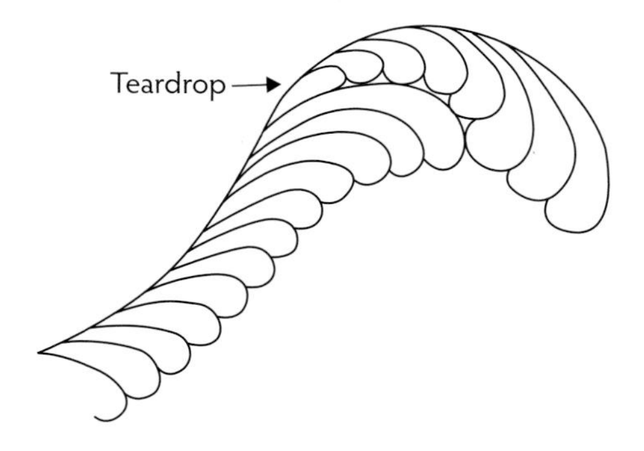

Better yet, add two!

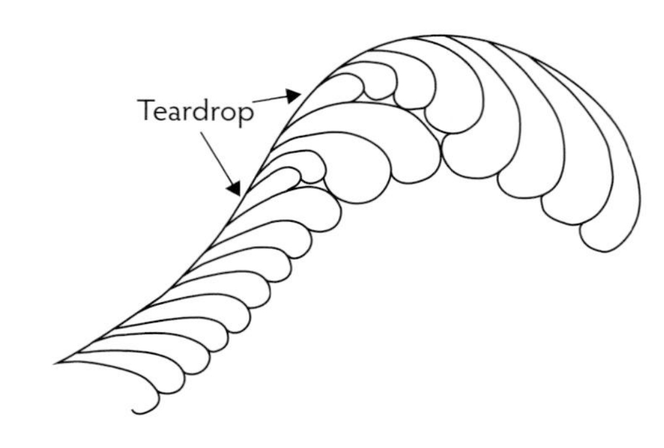

Notice how the teardrops add variety, giving the plume a flirty feel. While on my most formal designs I personally prefer not adding teardrops, I do love the way they look on a less-formal quilt.

Stitching feathers on the outside curve is much easier to deal with. The quills of the feathers never have to travel very far, so keeping the quills short is easy. As you follow the downward curve, make your feathers smaller and smaller, adding a "drip" off the end.

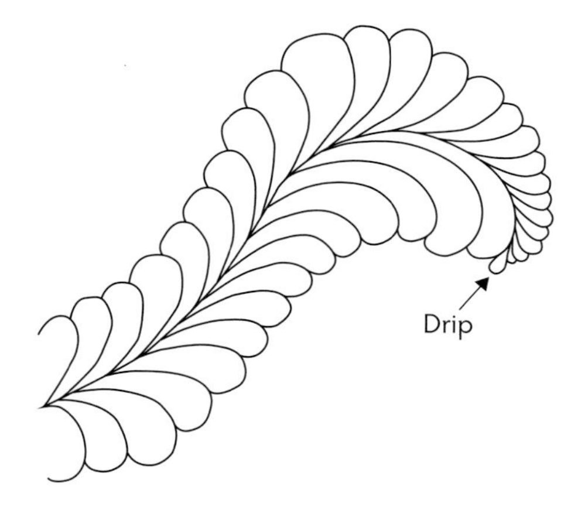

STEMLESS STITCHING

Stemless stitching of feathers is an important method for creating many of my semiformal designs. I use this method to create less thread buildup when traveling from one feather to the next and to keep a continuous thread path. Having a clearly *marked* stem on your quilt top is important for making feathers in this manner. The plumes are not literally stemless, but rather the feathers are stitched first, and the stem is added at the end as a way to travel to the next area of the quilt.

Start by marking the stem with your favorite marking tool. Being careful to use your chalked stem as if it were stitched, you'll then generally stitch two feathers to the left and two to the right. It will feel strange at first, bumping the end of your quill up to nothing but chalk; however, it gets easier with practice.

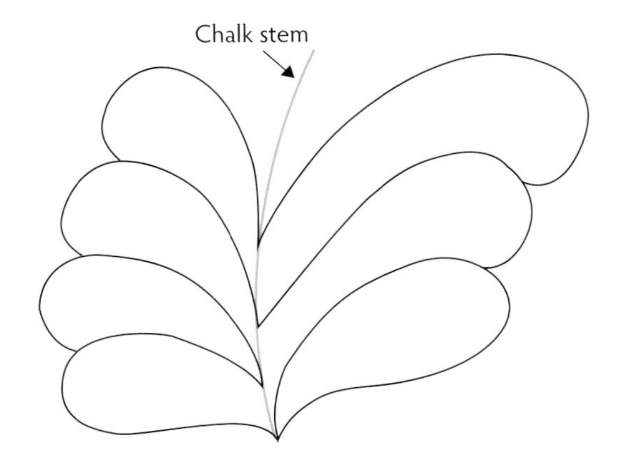

The thread path for stemless feathers is shown at right. Notice that you'll switch sides, stitching on opposite sides of the marked stem, depending on how long your quills become. As the quills become longer, switch sides.

On an outside curve, in order to keep your quills equal and not create any fingers, you'll need to make three to four feathers on one side of the marked stem and then return to stitching the two-per-side repeat.

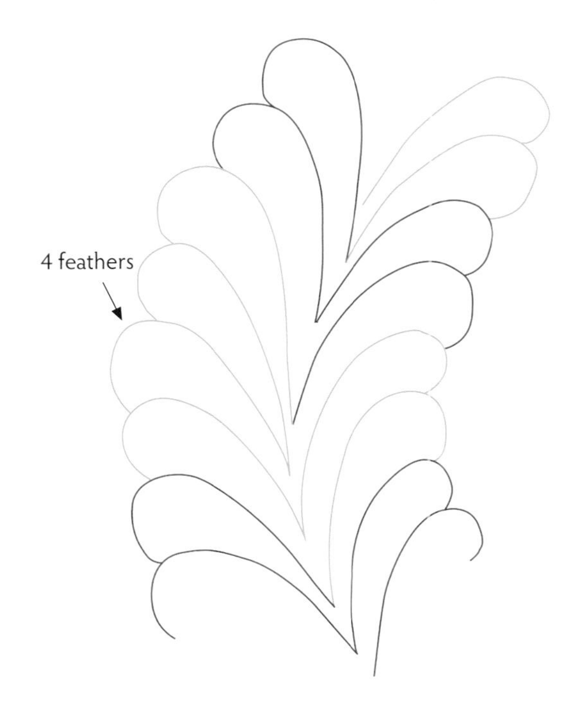

Using the color-coded example below, follow the path with your finger or pencil, starting with the red feathers. It won't take you long to get a feel for when you need to switch sides.

When you reach the end feather cap, you'll complete the plume by stitching the stem indicated in red below.

OPEN-QUILLED STITCHING

Stitching feathers using the open-quilled technique is another way to travel with your quilting stitches while cutting down on thread buildup. The method is similar to the stemless technique, but you stitch the feathers on one side of the plume at a time and then stitch the stem as a way to travel.

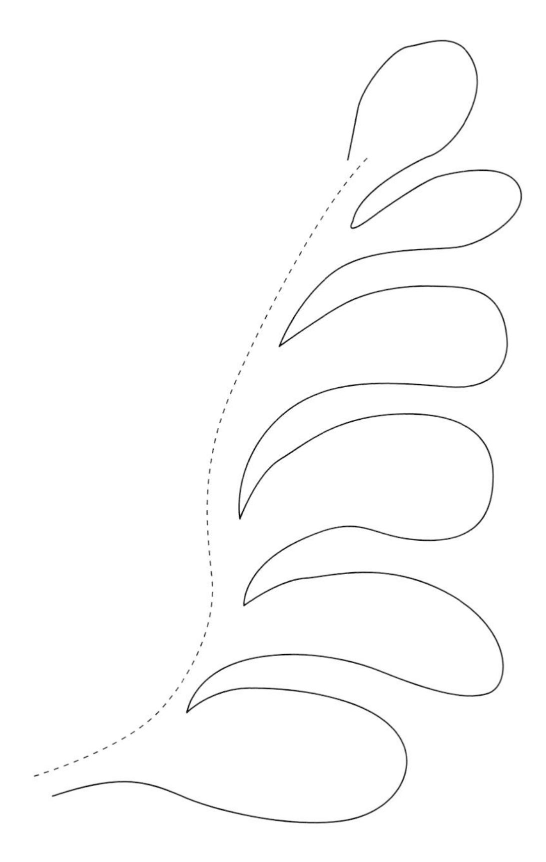

THE BASIC FEATHERS

In this section I show you how to make the three feather styles—long-arm, lace, and heirloom feathers. You'll use the same thread path for each. **Note:** In any drawing, a dashed line represents a chalked line or registration line.

The Long-Arm Feather

1. Mark the stem with chalk.
2. Starting at the base of your plume (stem), create open-quilled feathers to the right of the stem as shown. Stitch a teardrop at the top.

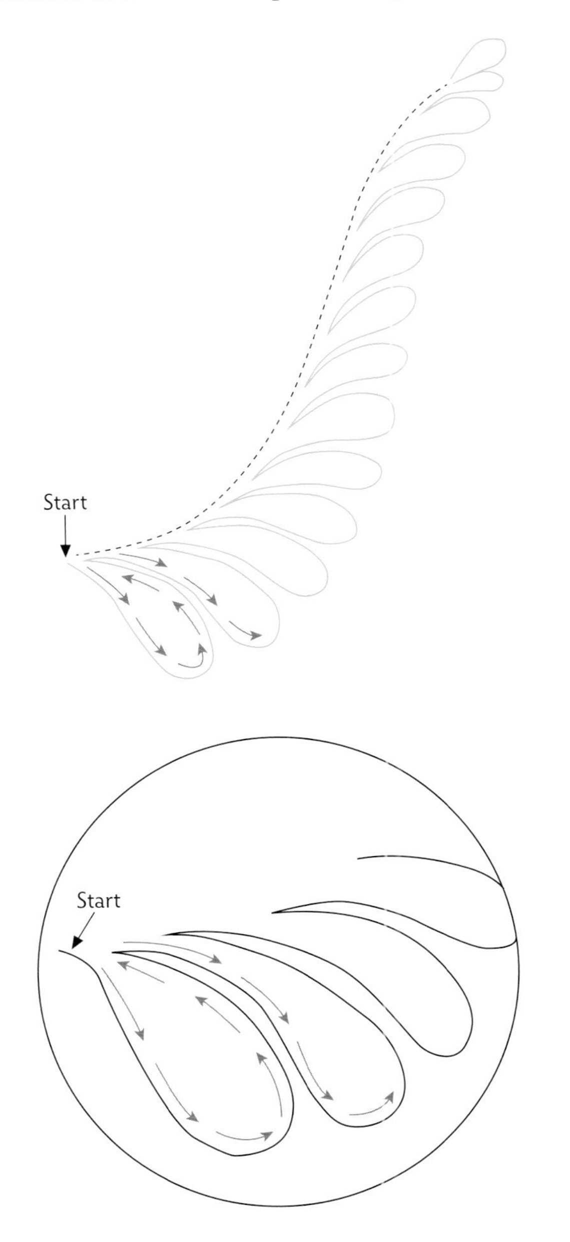

3. Stitch the stem by traveling along the open-quilled feathers and thereby closing them.

4. Stitch the feathers on the left of the stem and tie off at the tip.

The Lace Feather

The lace feather is made by creating a hook shape. Be careful to not let your hook cross over into the previous feather. The feather created under the hook (A) needs to be at least two-thirds the height of the full feathers.

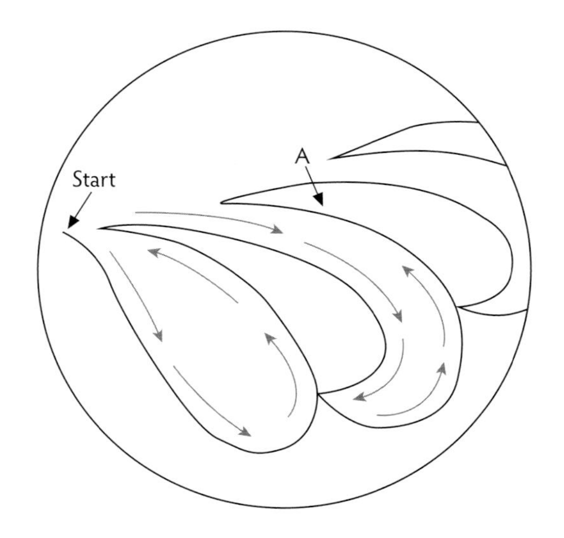

1. Chalk the stem and stitch lace feathers to the right, ending with a teardrop at the top.

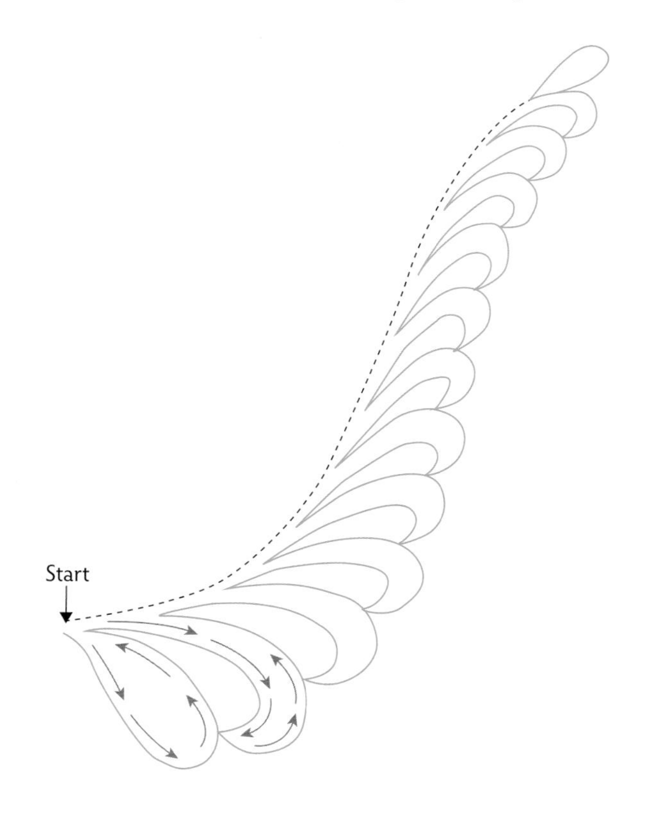

2. Stitch the stem to close the open-quilled lace feathers.

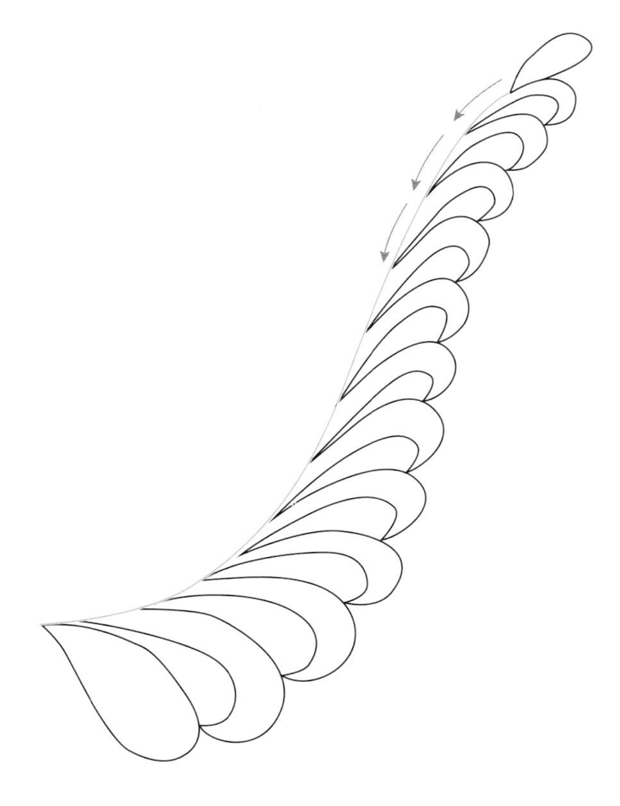

3. Stitch feathers on the left of the stem and tie off at the top.

Example of heirloom feathers

The Heirloom Feather

This feather is the hardest and takes the most practice due to backtracking (stitching over previous stitches precisely). The backtracking is done on every other feather cap. Don't worry if you don't hit the backtracking exactly at first. That will come with practice.

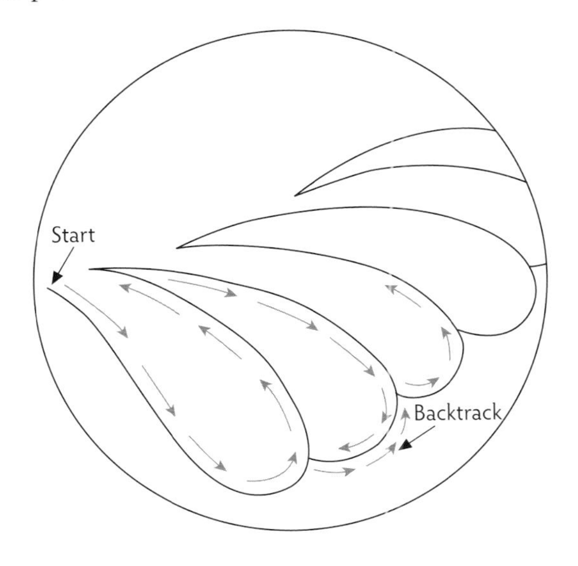

Key Point~Start Small

When learning to make heirloom feathers, it's better to start out with smaller feathers. The smaller size makes it easier to hit your previous stitching when backtracking.

1. Begin stitching at the base of the plume and create feathers to the right. Make a teardrop at the end.

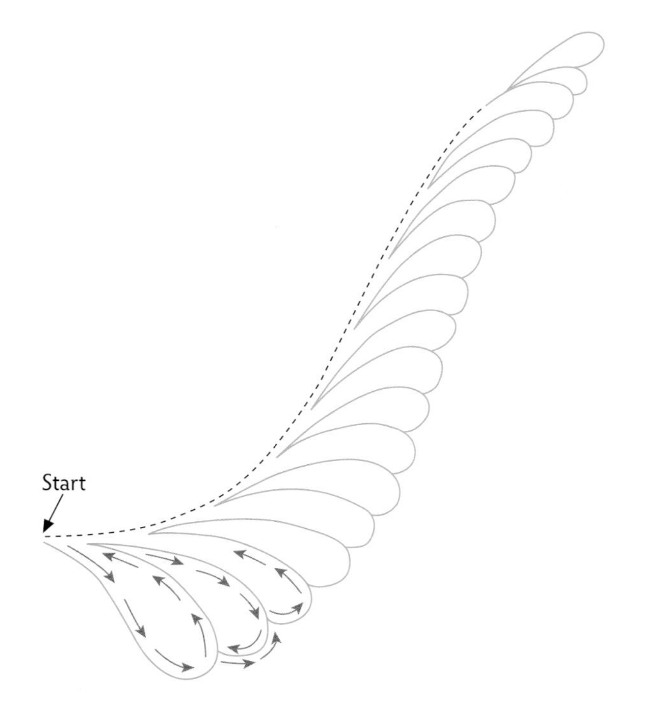

2. Travel down the stem line and stitch feathers up the left side. Tie off at the top.

Turning Border Corners

Turning corners on borders can leave you wondering why you ever took up this crazy hobby of quilting. It's not so bad with straight-line quilting designs such as piano keys (page 92) or beadboards (page 93), but if you want a curve in your border, such as serpentine feathers, feathered cable, or curling feathers, you'll need to spend some time to figure out a plan.

The way to deal with a meandering border design that requires the least amount of hair pulling is to simply end your border in the corner. Don't worry about it flowing around the turn. This is achieved by starting your border motif in the center and working your way outward in both directions.

However, if you want the design to be continuous, always keep in mind that you need a dip, or valley, before each corner, rather than an arch, or hill. For this to happen, you'll *always* need to have an odd number of hills and valleys. Count each hill and valley, add them up, and it needs to be an odd number. In other words, the total number of valleys will always be one more than the number of hills. If you have six hills, you'll need seven valleys; the total of both is 13, an odd number.

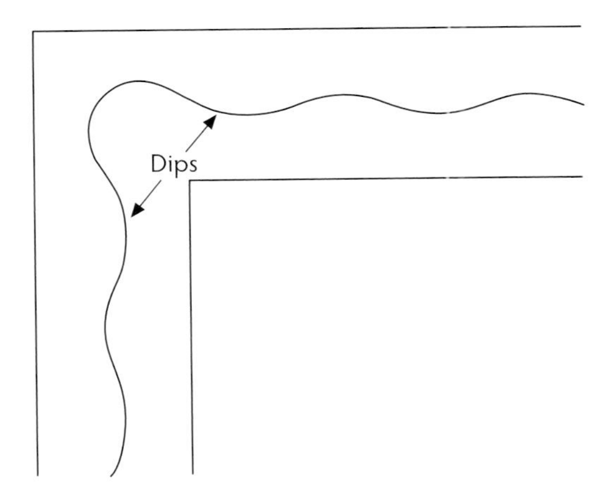

I know you're giggling now, because of course every border is the perfect length, and we always have an odd number of hills and valleys to make it around the corner. Let's collectively laugh. This would be why I wrote the next section on extensions. Be sure to read the section "Amish Curling Feathers" on page 48. That section walks you through the process of modifying your design to fit your specific border length.

Extensions

We're not talking hair, but rather extensions of designs to make the design fit the space. It requires the dreaded M word—math. Most of us hate it, but we all have to use it at some point. Who would have thought when we were taking algebra in high school that we'd actually put it to good use, let alone use it in quilting? But we do just that every time we piece a quilt or plan the quilting design.

ADDING TO THE APEX

Not all borders on every quilt are created equal. Worst-case scenario, none of the borders on an individual quilt are created equal. Let's take my award-winning quilt "Jelly-icious." I hate to admit it, but Jelly (my shorthand for "Jelly-icious") is not square. After I pieced the top, no two sides on this quilt were the same length.

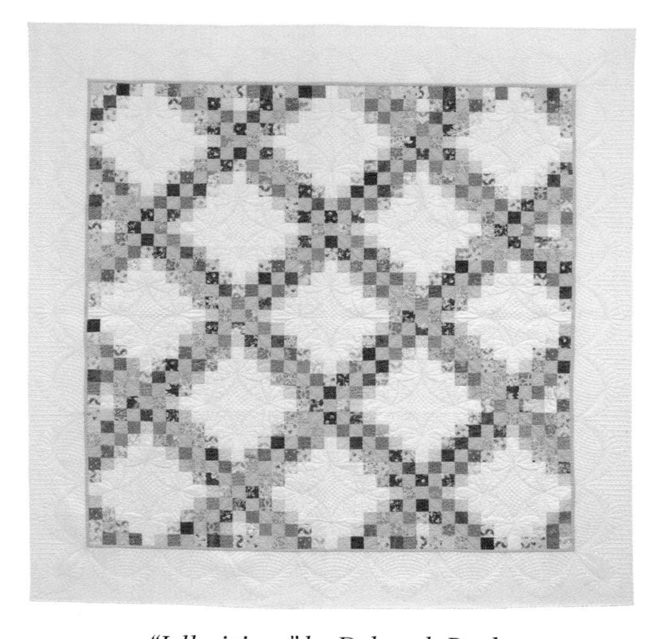

"Jelly-icious" by Deborah Poole

Close-up of "Jelly-icious" border design

Remember, perfection is an illusion. Let me say that again. Perfection is an illusion. Jelly's longest side is a full 2" longer than the shortest side. So how did I make the border motifs seem so perfect and equal in size? Simple—I fudged it.

Only one side on this quilt has arcs that all measure exactly 10". On the other sides they range from 10" to 10½" depending on how far off each border measurement was. The most important part of extending the arc is that you keep the apex of your curves the same height all the way across the border. Here are what the registration lines for Jelly's border look like.

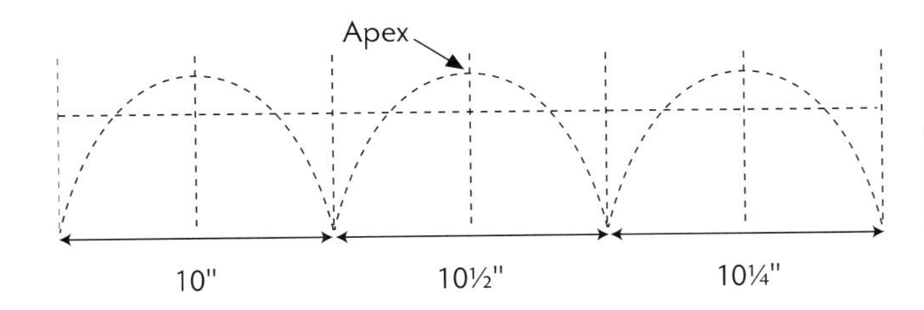

You want to keep the curve on the sides of your arcs the same. To do this, you need to keep the height of your apexes the same but also add the extra width to the apex, not just to the base of your arc. This is actually where the illusion of perfection comes in.

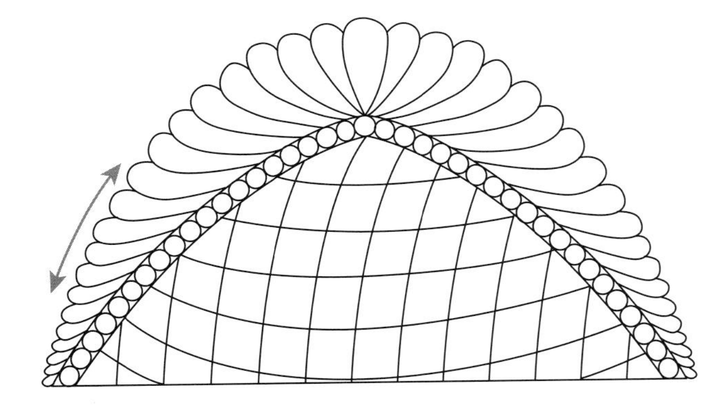

Now let's say that I needed to add as much as 1½" to an arc. (Yes, that's an exaggerated example, but I want it to be clear.) The illustration below shows what happens if you add the extra only to the base of the arc. The apex becomes flat and the sides become farther apart with less of a curve.

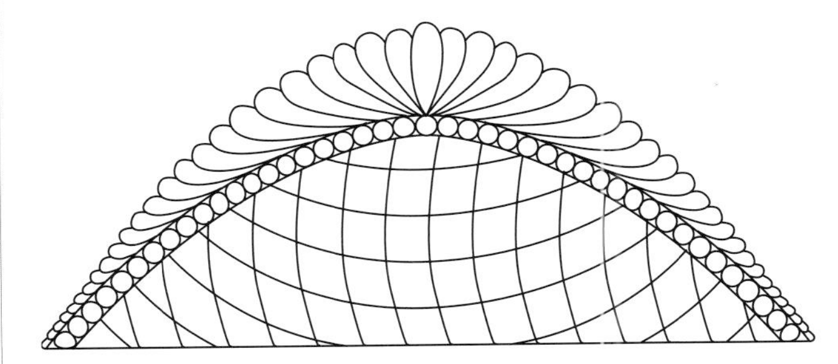

When you put the perfect 10" arc next to the 11½" arc with the width added to the base, you get an offset or skewed V between the arcs.

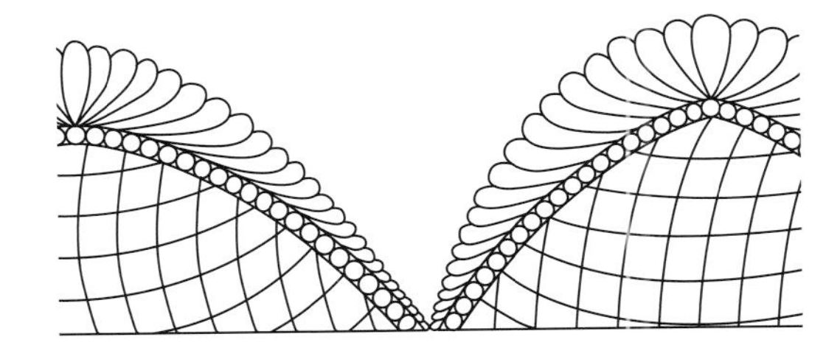

If you add the extra width to both the base *and* the apex, the difference is far less noticeable. The top of the arc becomes a little flatter, but the sides where each arc comes together have the same curve, so everything appears uniform.

To add extra width to the base and the apex, use your circle template to make the lower two-thirds of the curve the same. As you approach the apex, gently angle your template so that the arc along the top flattens out a bit, and stitch to the topmost point. Do the same on the opposite side. This will keep the angle and curves the same where the two motifs come together. The tops will be less round than others, but this won't be noticeable because the height is consistent.

AMISH CURLING-FEATHER EXTENSIONS

While Jelly's border was possible to extend, each motif had to be uniform. For serpentine or curling feather designs, it's much easier to make adjustments because you don't really need to evenly distribute excess length over the entire border as with the border design for Jelly. You can often add the extra length to only one or two motifs because the shape of the plume hides it so well. Count yourself lucky if your border measures only a little less or a little more than the coveted odd number of hills and valleys (discussed earlier in "Turning Border Corners," page 29). But don't be disheartened if that's not the case.

Close-up of the border of "Plain Jane," featured in Homestyle Quilts *by Kim Diehl and Laurie Baker (Martingale, 2012). Pieced by Barbara Walsh and Kim Diehl. Machine quilted by Deborah Poole.*

This is the registration line of the main stem of the Amish curling feather and where you'll make your extensions. (See "Amish Curling Feathers" on page 48.)

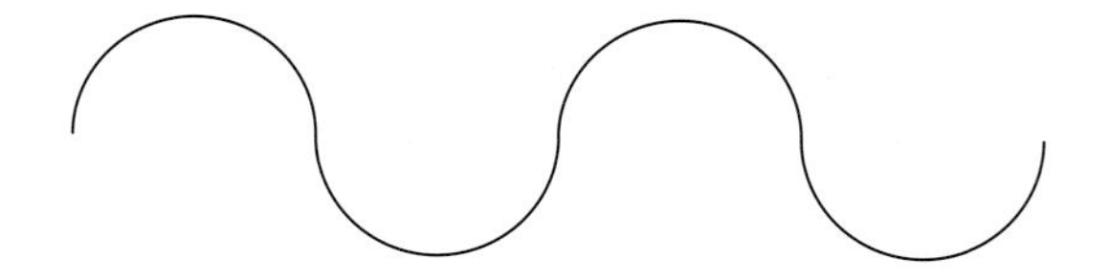

Unless I'm working with Amish curling feathers smaller than 4" (the diameter of the circle used to create the curl), I'll add as much as 2" to the apex of any curve. So if you only have to add 2" total, don't worry about adjusting each curl; you can simply add it all to the last curl. Again, the example below is exaggerated to make the point. This same process will hold true for serpentine feathers and feathered cables included in the section "Traditional Designs" beginning on page 42.

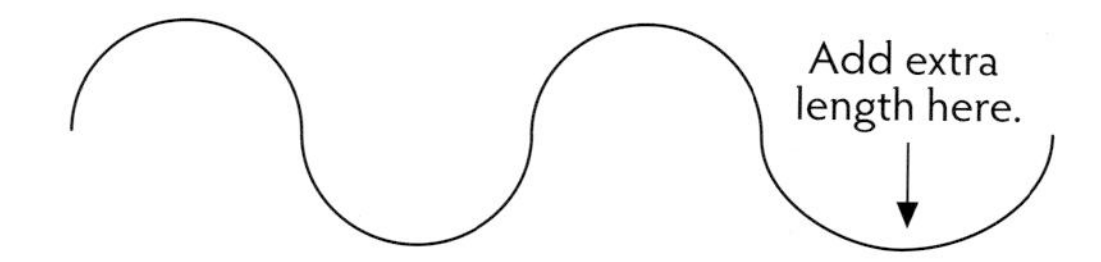

MAKING IT ODD

So what do you do if you aren't so lucky and the length of your border dictates that you end up with an even number of hills and valleys? Easy—divide the width of your extra hill by the desired total number of hills and valleys. As an example, let's say you have eight hills and valleys that are 10" wide and you need to make it seven. Divide 10" by 7, and that gives you roughly 1½". You need to add 1½" to each of the seven hills and valleys. It will make your curls a little less round or your arcs a little flatter, but I promise no one will notice. There will be more on this in "Amish Curling Feathers" on page 48.

Use the same methods to lengthen or shorten any curved border design, such as Amish curling feathers, serpentine feathers, or feathered cables.

Curved Crosshatching

This fairly simple design takes a quilt above and beyond formal and launches it into show quality. A little curved crosshatching (CCH) can add so much to traditional patchwork. Take the blue-and-white "Wedding Quilt", below, for example.

"Wedding Quilt" by Editha Van Orden. Machine quilted (original designs) by Deborah Poole. Owned by Melissa Borders. Quilt pattern is "Duty, Honor, Country," designed by Kelly Corbridge and originally published in McCall's Quilting, *February 2005.*

This quilt is stunning on any level with its high-contrasting color scheme, but the quilting takes it over the top, largely, in my opinion, due to the curved crosshatching. In the photo at right, you can see how curved crosshatching gave a simply pieced block the "Wow!" factor.

Curved crosshatching is used in both the pieced blocks and alternate plain blocks.

Review the steps that follow, and after some practice, you'll easily get an A in curved crosshatching. I use circle and oval templates as a guide when stitching curved crosshatching. The photographs included here show an oval template. Use the etched lines on your template to create your spacing.

If your template didn't come with ¼" markings, you'll need to mark your own. Using a fine-line permanent marker, draw lines through the center of your template, dividing it in half vertically and horizontally to create a 90° angle at the center. Beginning at one of those lines and using a straight-edge ruler with ¼" markings, draw lines across one side of your template ¼" apart.

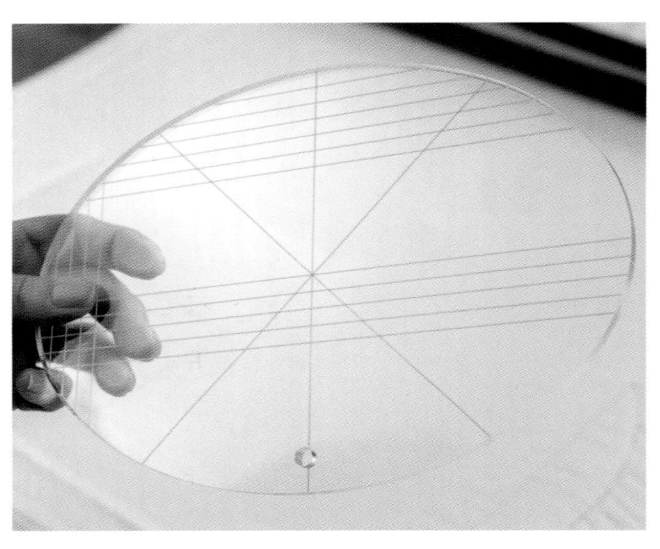

Oval template with etched markings

1. Always mark 90°-angle registration lines through the center of the block or space.

Mark registration lines.

2. Place the 90° line of your circle or oval on the registration line of your square so that your first stitching line will begin and end in the corners. Beginning in the lower-left corner, stitch the first arc and continue around the block to stitch an arc on all four sides.

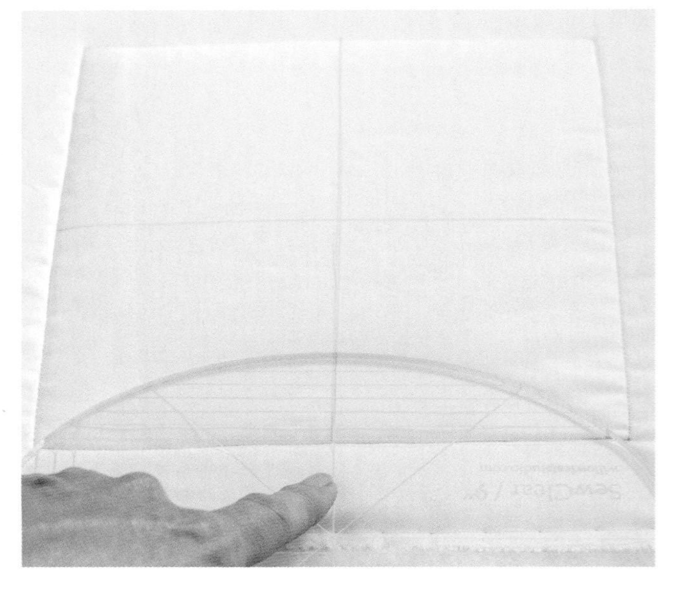

Template placement for the first line of stitching

3. Align the 90° line on your oval or circle with the 90° registration line marked on your quilt to keep your crosshatching even and uniform. If you're off even slightly by the time you get to the other side of your square, your spacing will be wonky, large on one side and small on the other. Correct alignment of the template is very important for successful CCH.

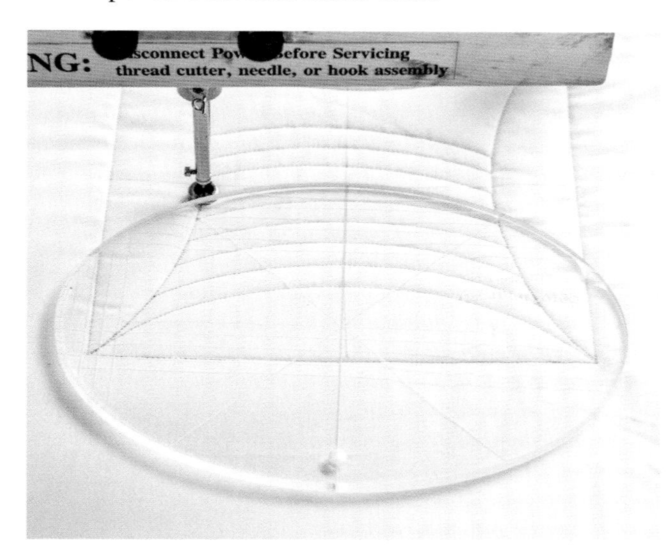

Template is not aligned with registration lines.

Results are skewed stitching lines.

Curved crosshashing adds extra zing to any motif.

4. Begin stitching in the lower-left corner and work your way back and forth across the block. Travel up the first stitched lines to the next line to be stitched. I usually stitch the curves ½" apart, but depending on the quilt, the lines may be as much as 1" apart (fig. 1).
5. Stitch the arcs in the opposite direction, creating what I call the cross section (fig. 2).

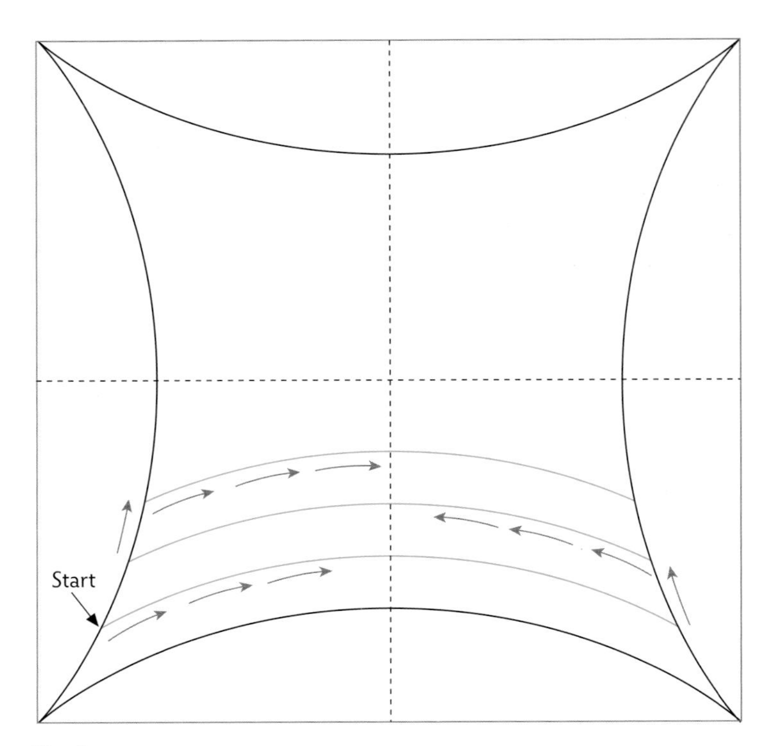

Fig. 1

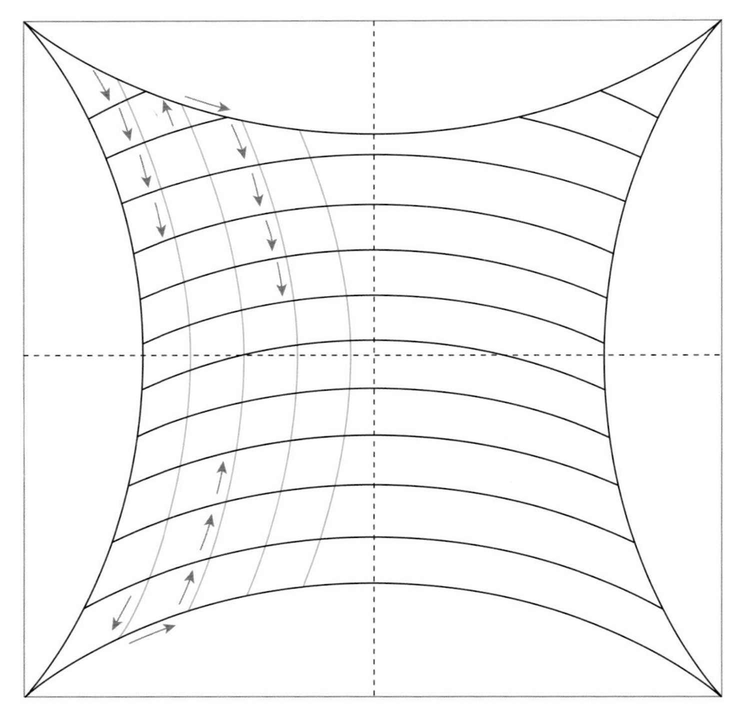

Fig. 2

No matter what shape the design is, mark registration lines to create the 90° angle for curved crosshatching. With the heart shape at right, your stitching will travel over the previously stitched feathers to move to the next line (fig. 3).

I like to draw out my designs first, previewing which direction to place my 90° registration lines. A good example of what happens if you don't make registration lines or preview their direction is shown in figure 4.

Fig. 3

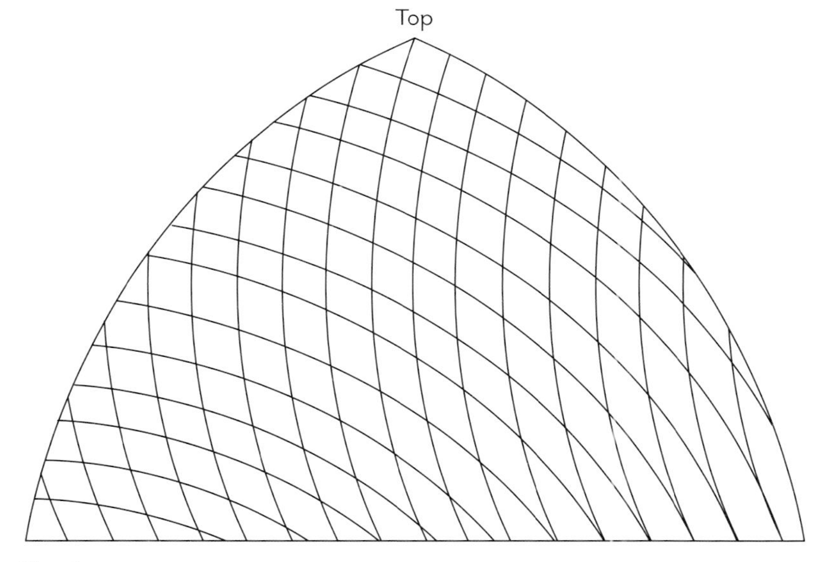

Fig. 4

Key Point~Partial Crosshatching

When stitching curved crosshatching, you don't always have to fill the entire space in both directions. Try crossing just a few lines, creating sub-patterns within the space.

Channels and Pearls

I use what most in the industry call "channels" and "pearls" to make my designs continuous while avoiding thread buildup from backtracking. Heirloom quilting is very dense, usually containing lots of feathers, crosshatching, and fine background fills. While heirloom quilting often requires backtracking, channels and pearls help alleviate that need while giving the stitched design a continuous thread path and added detail.

CHANNELING

Quilting a channel is really quite easy. The simplest way to describe a channel is to say it's an echo-quilting line spaced ¼" from a previous line. Channeling can be used on any stem. Channels raise a feathered wreath a step above the rest.

Feathered wreath with a channel

You can stop and start at each stem, but I usually make the inner circle first, feather to the inside, stitch a straight line across the ¼" spacing to create the outer circle of the channel, and then feather the outside. For a typical quilt, that little line in the channel never shows enough to matter. However, if it's a show quilt, I'll stop and start each circle.

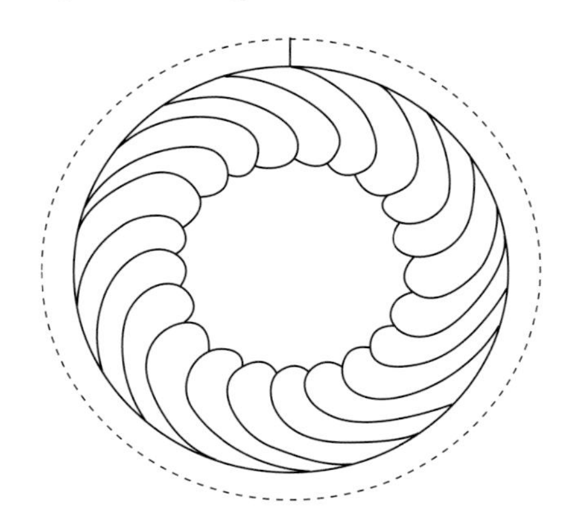

Notice how in the illustration below, the line used to jump the channel is visible, yet it isn't really *that* noticeable. If your fabric and thread match, the line won't be noticed at all in the finished quilt.

PEARLING

While a channel can take a feathered wreath the extra mile, adding pearls in that channel turns that same wreath into a superstar.

Again I start by stitching the inner ring and feathering it. But instead of making a straight line to the outer ring, I stitch a single pearl, create the channel, feather the outer ring, and then come back to stitch pearls in the channel.

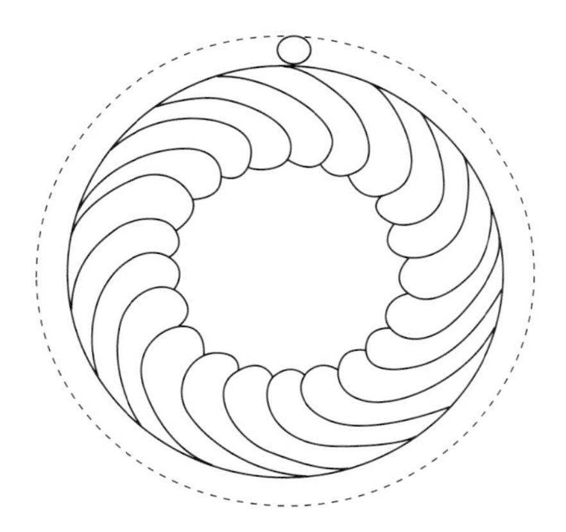

If you have a really large space, like the corner squares on a Star of Bethlehem quilt, and want to take your wreath over the top, create a wreath within a wreath.

MAKING THE PEARLS ROUND

Most often, pearls are only ¼" in diameter, but I have quilted several quilts using ½" pearls. One of the questions I'm asked over and over is, "How do you get your pearls so round?" The first answer (which you're not going to like) is that it takes a lot of PPPing. There are well over 10,000 pearls in the "Wedding Quilt" alone (page 104).

Second, slow down when stitching. To help do that, put some weight on your throat plate. Be that a bag of rice or lowering the take-up bar to rest on the throat plate, extra weight will add control to anything you do.

The last answer—while this may sound silly or even a little insulting, it's the truth—is that you have to consciously *think* about making pearls round. For an award-winning quilt, you can't run ahead and think about getting to the end of the channel, what to add to your shopping list, or even the words to the song you're listening to. You have to think about each and every pearl. The instant you stop giving every pearl the attention of a jealous lover is when they become flat on one side.

Quarter-Inch Pearls

However, there's light at the end of this pearly spinning tunnel. Unless you're entering your quilt in a national show, don't worry about making your pearls all perfectly round. That's right, *don't worry!* Refer back to my earlier statement: "Perfection is an illusion." The same goes for ¼" round pearls—they're an illusion. So what, if some are round (and believe me, some will be); some are flat on one side (yes again, some will be); and some are almost square. It does not matter. The overall effect is going to be the same as if every pearl were perfectly round.

To further the illusion of perfection, I use my Bohin pencil to mark the first few pearls in the registration lines before stitching. I also mark those pearls in valleys and intersections (the areas in the red circles below) so that the pearls in those more obvious places will look the same.

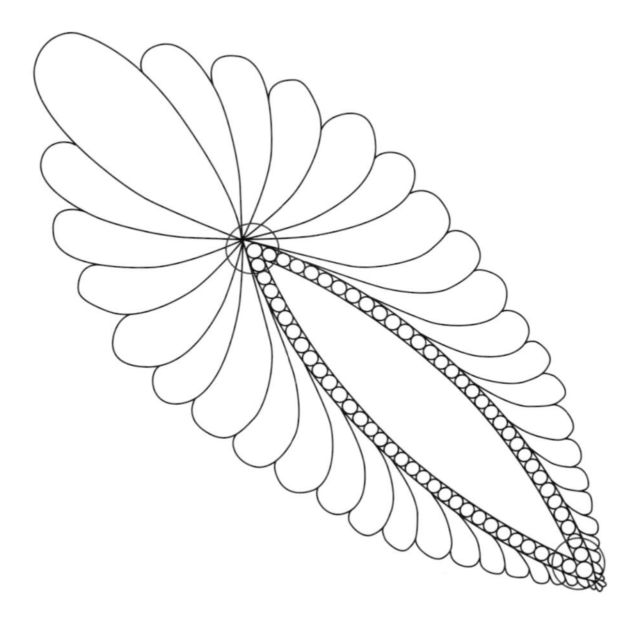

Half-Inch Pearls

Unfortunately, illusion is *not true* for ½" pearls. Remember the superstar status of ¼" pearls? Well, ½" pearls can be deemed the crown jewels and should be treated as such. In the design for my award-winning quilt "Dresden's Dilemma," I believe the ½" pearls were the key to its success.

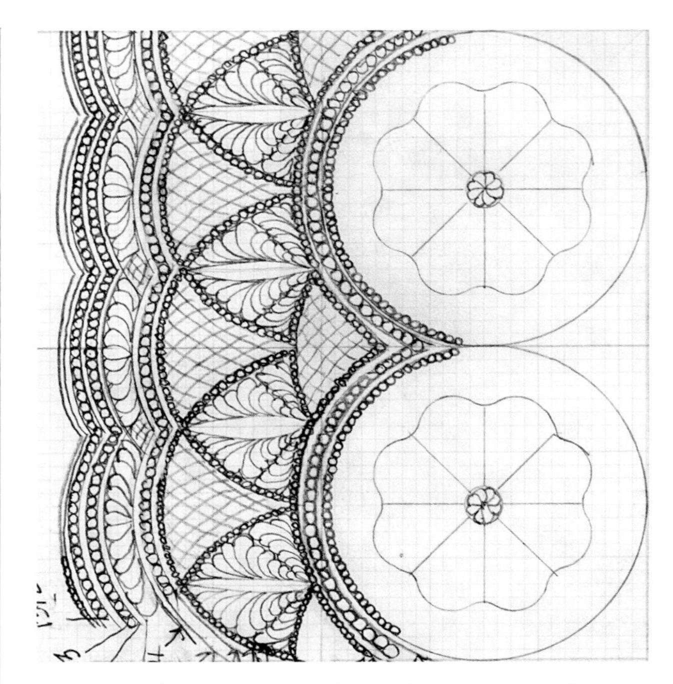

Drafted design for "Dresden's Dilemma"

Border design for "Dresden's Dilemma"

While I stitched many of the ½" pearls completely freehand on "Dresden's Dilemma," they just weren't round enough for my liking, so I finally broke down and started marking each ½" circle with an architectural circle template (shown on page 14). I recommend marking ½" pearls if you want them nice and round and don't want to be tearing out your hair—or your stitches!

PEARLING TECHNIQUES

I always create a stitched channel to hold the pearls. I have tried chalking the channel, but I never seem to be able to keep the pearls inside a channel that hasn't been stitched. You can try with or without. There are several techniques for creating pearls. I suggest you try each and find the one that suits you best. What is successful for me may not be for you. I know quilters who each use one of these different techniques, and all are successful.

Figure Eight

The figure eight, as its name suggests, is made by stitching rounded, undulating curves across the channel in one direction and then the other. I know quite a few machine quilters who have great success with this method.

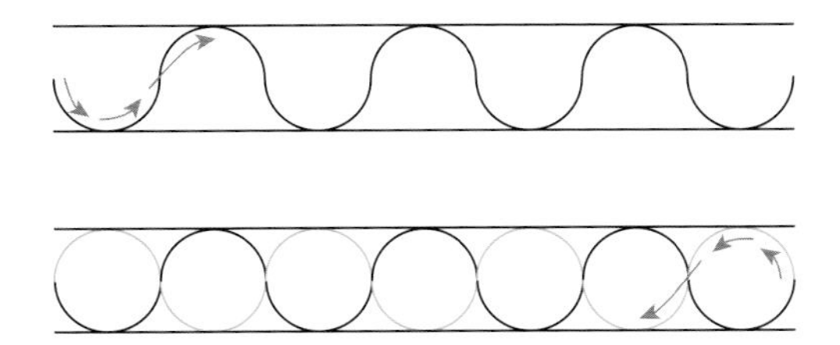

Os

Os are exactly that—a continuous line of lowercase letter *o* shapes. You use the edge of the channel to travel. I like to stitch these on the inside curves of motifs such as hearts. The hard part to this is making them really round and not *e*-like.

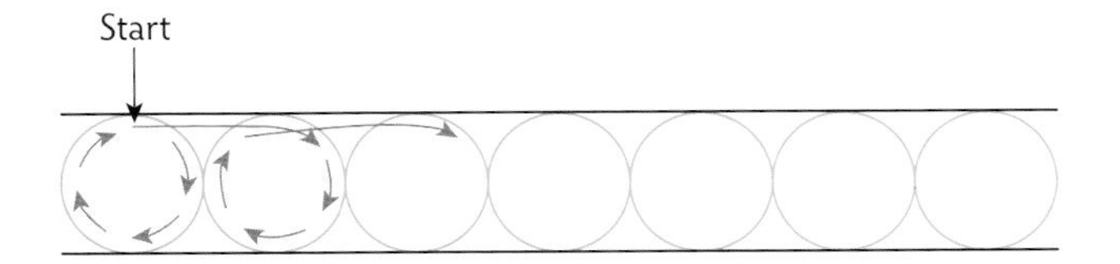

Bump It

Bumps are half pearls made in the channel by stitching scallops, or half circles, in one direction and then back. The trick to this pearl is making your bumps match and stitching only halfway across the channel. While I do know quilters who use this technique with success, it is my least-favorite method.

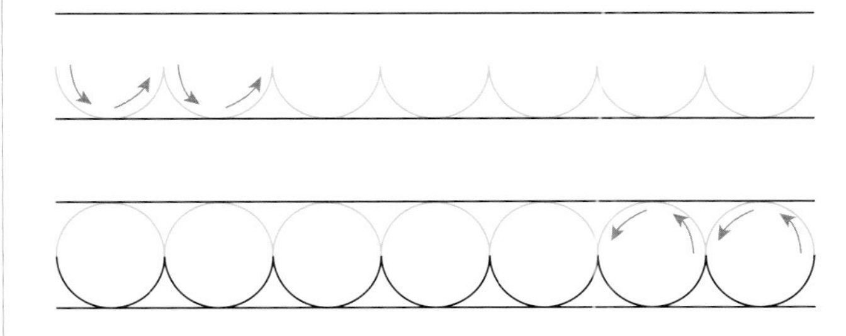

One-and-a-Half Rounds

This is the method I use the most. You stitch a complete circle, then travel over the top half of the circle and stitch your next pearl (A). Travel over the bottom half of this pearl to begin the next pearl (B). Repeat across the channel. Essentially, you are backtracking over half of each circle, alternating between the top and bottom halves.

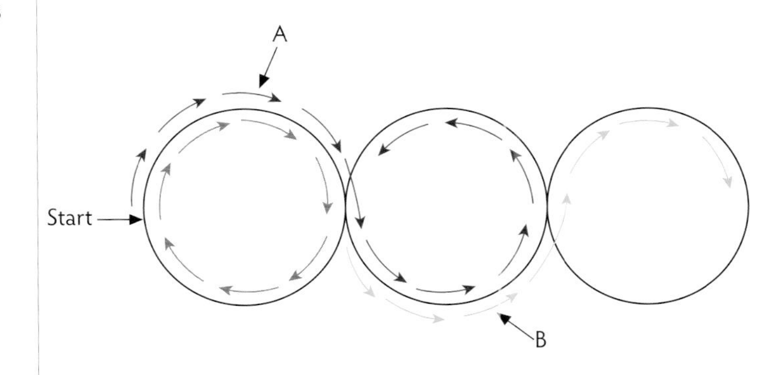

And now the part you've truly been waiting for—how to put all that you've learned in the previous sections into a design. But please bear with me just a little longer while I explain how these designs work.

A NOTE ABOUT THE DESIGNS

I specialize in taking a complicated design and creating a thread path with one start and one stop. I hate tying off and starting again.

For each design, there is a drawing of the final motif. Then there is a line diagram of the registration lines and a color-coded step-by-step continuous thread path. The registration lines are shown as dashed lines. *Be sure to compare the registration lines to the actual thread path.* Unless the registration line is also the stem of a feather, in most cases you *don't stitch on the registration line;* you only stitch up to it. Keep that in mind as you mark your quilt. I've said this before, but in case you missed it, *registration lines are the finished edge of the motif.* Think of registration lines as a wall you want to bump up against.

SERPENTINE FEATHERS

For the thread path of this design, refer to the instructions for stemless feathers on page 23 or open-quilled feathers on page 25, depending on the style of feather that you choose.

The marking for this design is easy. First mark a center line through your border. If you want the feathers to fill the border from side to side (fig. 1), mark the stem as shown below.

If you want the feathers to curve through the border, or wave (fig. 2), mark the stem and the two outer registration lines as shown below.

Fig. 1 Fig. 2

FEATHERED WREATH

A feathered wreath can be stitched using either the stemless (page 23) or open-quilled (page 25) feather methods, but the stem will always be stitched first. The real trick to making a good feathered wreath is to get the angle of your inner feathers correct (A).

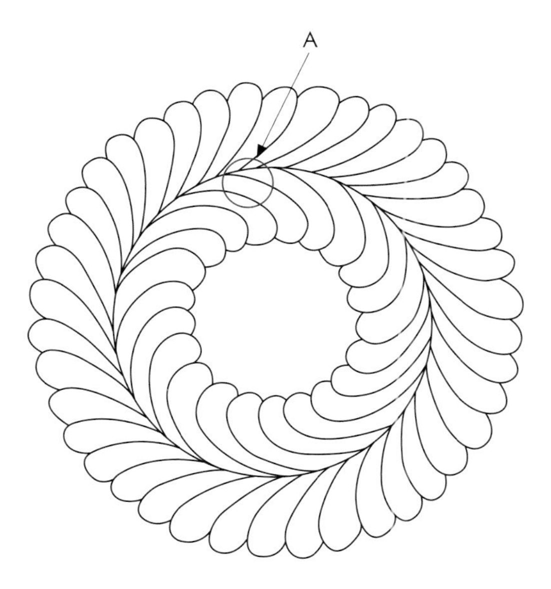

For some reason, it's hardest to get the correct angle of a feather on the inner circle of a wreath. Many people, myself included when I first started, tend to angle the feather downward rather than to the side.

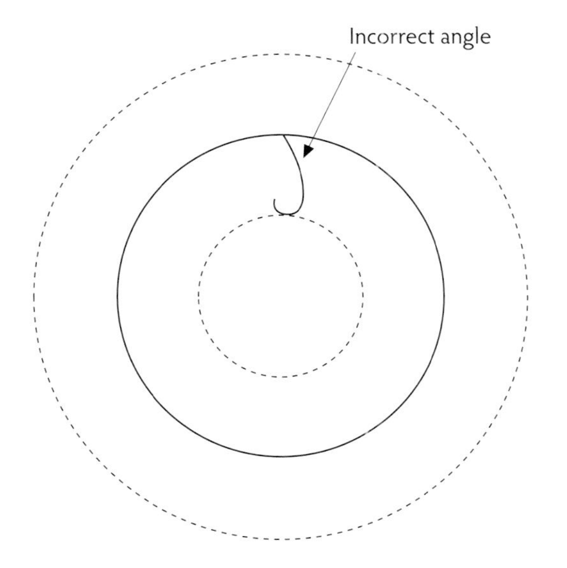

If you angle the feathers downward instead of to the side, you're in trouble from the first feather. You want the inside of the wreath to *swirl*, and if the first feather doesn't move along the curve, you'll need to rip it out and start over so you don't end up with something like what's shown below.

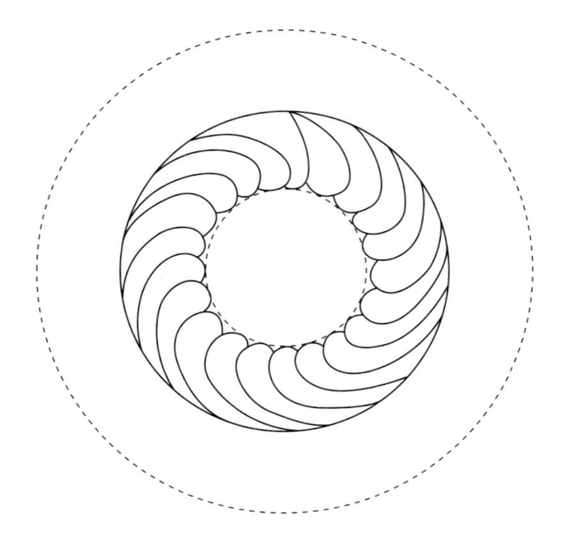

Think of your wreath as a clock. I always start my feathers at twelve o'clock, begin my first angle toward three o'clock, and then finish the curl of the feather at five. It will seem uncomfortable at first, but I promise if you angle that first feather correctly, your wreaths will always have that great swirl we love so much.

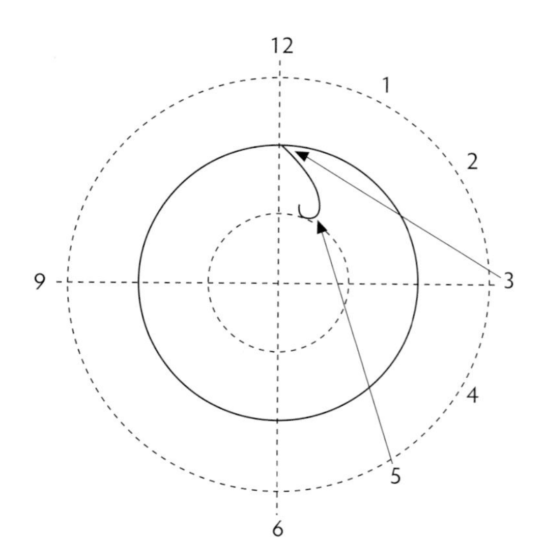

Determine the diameter for your wreath based on the space it will fill. I like a two-thirds ratio for most wreaths, meaning that the diameter of the stem circle is two-thirds of the diameter of the finished wreath. The registration lines for the inner circle would be one-third of the diameter of the finished wreath. Let's say you want a 9" wreath; the outer diameter would be 9" and the inner diameter would be 3". Draw these circles as your registration lines. Remember when marking the registration lines for this design that they are the *finished edge* of the wreath. For the stem, you will use your circle template to stitch a 6"-diameter circle.

Key Point~Larger Wreaths

For a 12"-diameter wreath, your stem would be an 8"-diameter circle, and the center circle will be 4" in diameter. For circles this large, you will need to consider adding stitching such as crosshatching to the center space.

1. Mark the middle of your square by chalking horizontal and vertical lines at a 90° angle. Place your circle templates on the lines to mark the inner and outer circles. This is another reason why I like solid circle templates rather than nesting circle templates (which are like rings). It's easy to align the etched lines on your circle templates with the chalked right angle to keep everything centered.

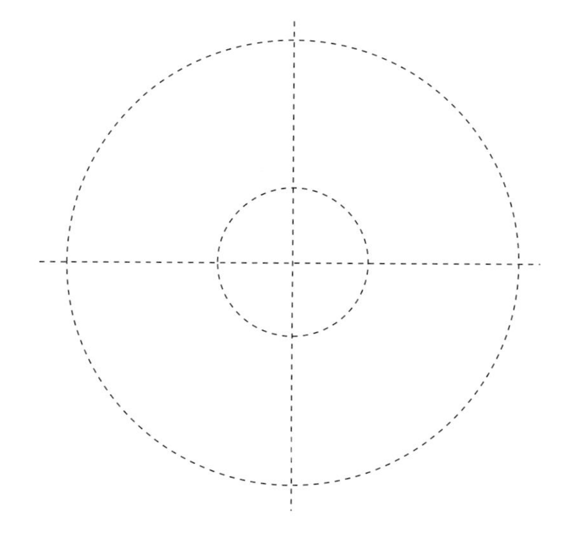

2. Using your circle template to guide your hopping foot, stitch the stem. To determine the size of the circle template, subtract ½" from the finished diameter of your stem. For a home sewing machine, mark the stem circle.

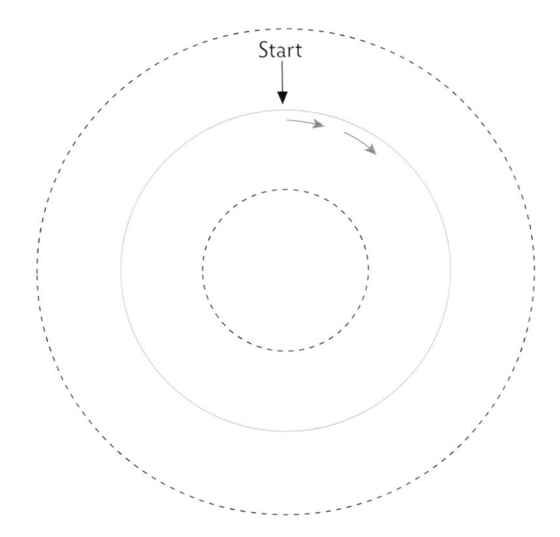

3. Stitch the outside feathers first, beginning at the top of the stem. This is not a hard-and-fast rule. I always stitch the outside feathers first, but you can begin in the center if you prefer.

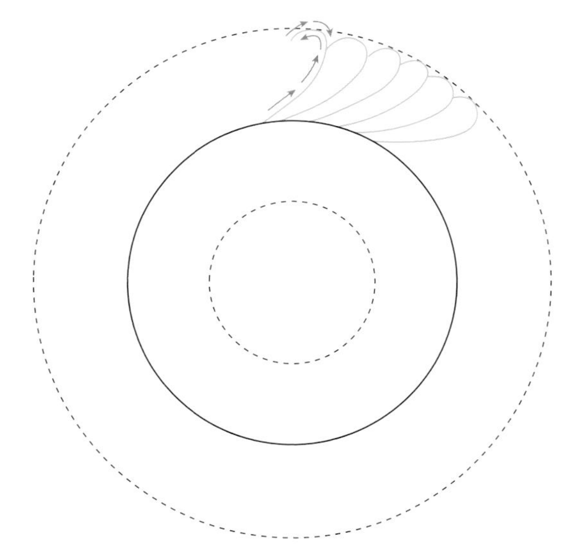

4. Finish by stitching the inside feathers.

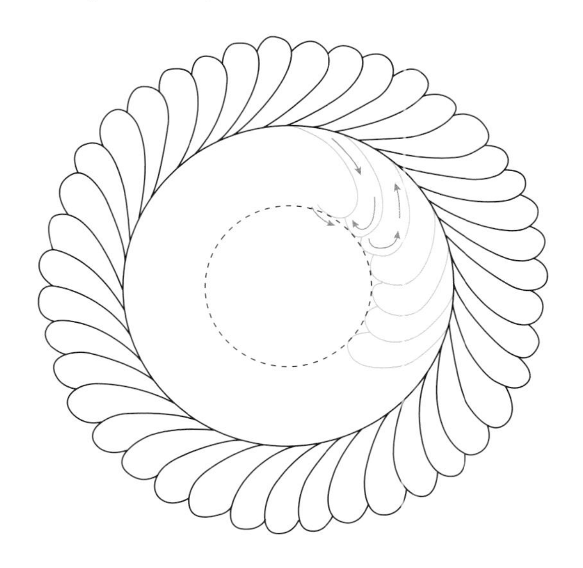

Feathered wreaths don't always have to go in open spaces.

FEATHERED CABLE

You'll make the feathered cable using the stemless-feather method on page 23. The easiest way to mark the feathered cable is to purchase a ready-made plain cable stencil. After you have one, it's easy to make your own stencils in different sizes using the purchased one as a guide.

1. Use the stencil to mark the stem and outer registration lines. If your stencil doesn't fit the length of your border perfectly, refer to "Extensions" on page 30 to fit the design to the space. The same methods apply to stencils. When placing your stencil for marking, you will want the stem lines to meet in the center, forming two almond shapes, facing in opposite directions.

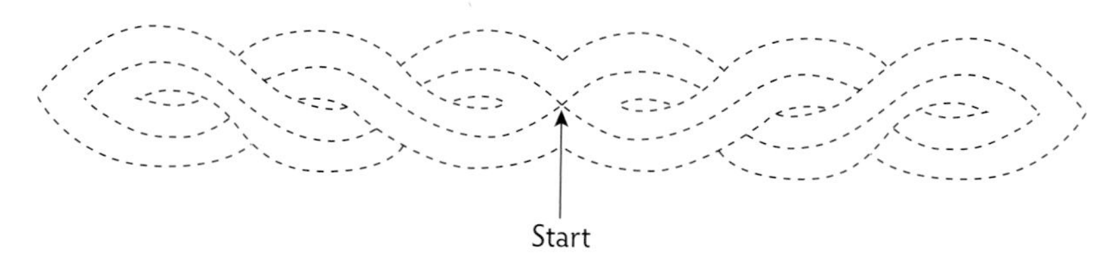

Feathered cable in a wide border

2. Begin stitching in the center of the cable, making two figure eights.

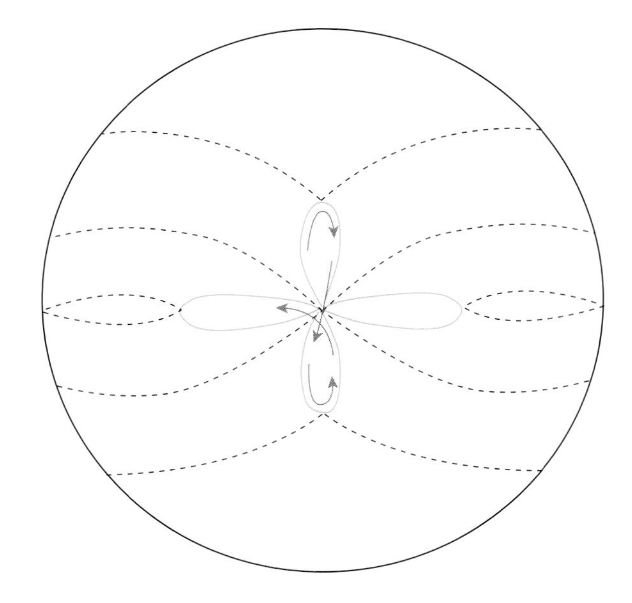

3. Using the stemless-feather method, travel toward the right to the first crossover.

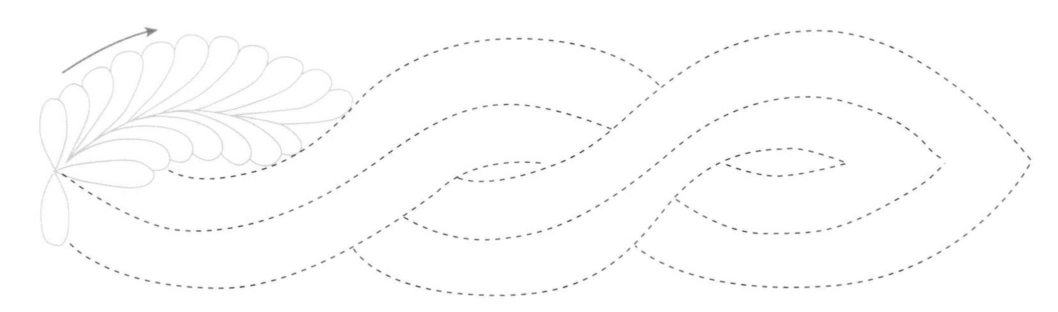

4. Travel to the left to create the stem on the upper portion of the cable, and then stitch the next set of feathers to the right, as far as the next crossover.

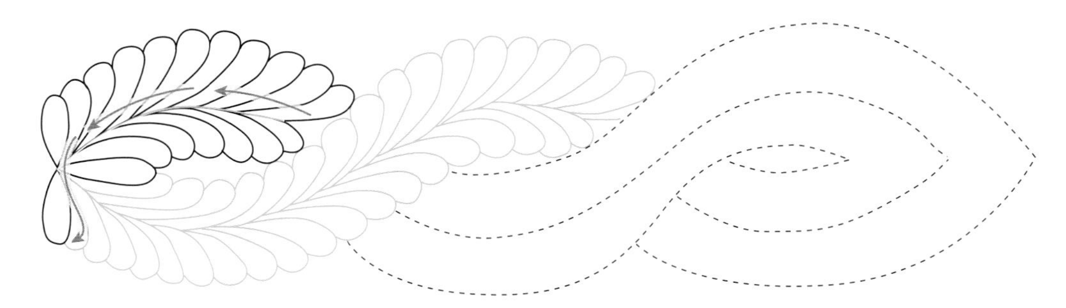

5. Repeat step 4 to the end of your cable, adding a drip or cap at the end.

6. Travel left again to stitch the stem on the bottom feathers back to the starting point. Repeat the stitching in the opposite direction to complete the left half of the cable.

AMISH CURLING FEATHERS

I hope you're drooling, because curling feathers are probably my favorite border treatment. When a client brings me a quilt with a wide border made of a solid or tone-on-tone fabric, I start to salivate and know it's going to get a curling feather design, using one of the three styles of feather—heirloom, long-arm, or lace.

Amish curling feathers that fill border

Amish curling feathers that begin in center

Amish curling feathers corner

Amish curling feathers that curve

Let's look first at the parts of the feather and the registration lines. The curling feather has the most complicated registration lines. The curve is the main serpentine stem line. Think of the curls as the part of the feather that "curls back" from the main stem.

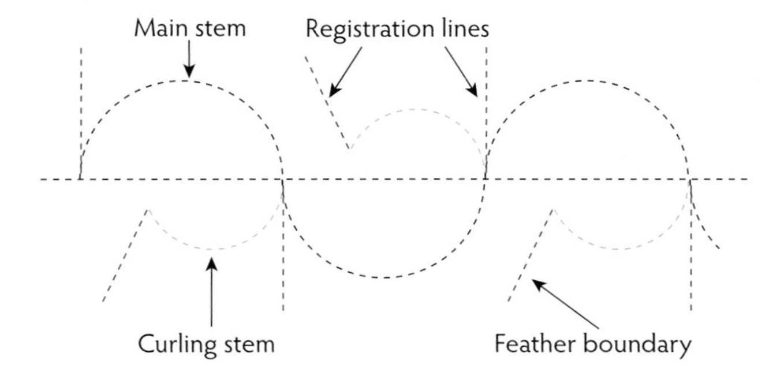

Note: This design is achieved completely freehand, meaning that no templates, pantographs, or computer are used to guide the stitching. Use your ¼"-thick circle templates for marking—not for guiding your hopping foot.

Determining Size of Curves and Curls

The first thing you need to do to make curling feathers is determine the size of the curves. This will help you establish how many hills and valleys you'll need to turn the corner if you're having them flow around the quilt. I like a two-thirds ratio or close to it—that means that the diameter of the curve is two-thirds the width of the border. Let's say we have a border that's 6" wide.

The main stem circle is easy: 6" x ⅔ = 4". That means we'll use a 4" circle to make the main stem or curve of the curling feather plume. However, 4" x ⅔ = 2.66" for the curling stem. Since this isn't a fraction we can measure with a ruler, we'll need to round up or round down. If I were new to making curling feathers, I'd chalk it out and see what looks best to me, but I know from doing too many of these to count that I'm going to round up to a 3" circle for the curling stem.

Calculating the Hills and Valleys

Let's say our 6"-wide border is 78" long. This will complicate things a bit, as you'll see later. The 4" curve of the main stem will determine the number of hills and valleys. The length of the border minus the corners is 66". We divide 66" by 4", the size of the main curve circles, and we get 16.5. That is the total number of hills and valleys. Everybody, now—groan. Not only do we have a dreaded even number of hills and valleys, it's a fraction as well. But not all is as bad as it seems.

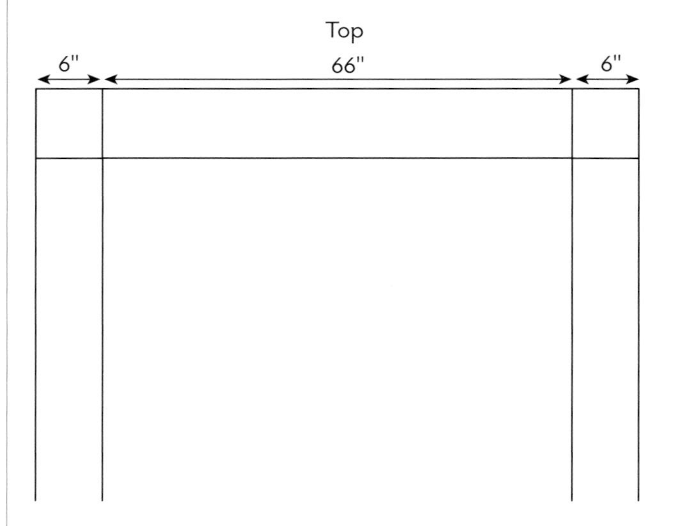

Remember, I intentionally made this difficult so you can learn what to do in this type of situation. You have two choices. The easiest choice, and the one I'd use on larger stems (6" and up), is to squeeze in another valley. So how do we do that? You're thinking magic, right? Not really. It's just simple math. We subtract from one to add to the other. We have a half valley that equals 2", so all we really need to do is find another 2" to squeeze in a complete 4" valley. In theory, that's doable. By shortening the apex of four hills and valleys by ½" each, we would free up 2" (4" x .5 = 2"). We would end up with the coveted odd number of 17 hills and valleys.

In reality, the reason we can't just rob Peter to pay Paul, so to speak, to get our 17 hills and valleys in this example is because our original 4" curve isn't that big, considering we've chosen 3" as our curl size. Even if we were to spread the needed 2" over all of the hills and valleys, a 1" spread between the curl and main stem doesn't leave much space to feather. So, we're going to have to decrease the number of hills and valleys to the next smaller odd number, 15.

Remember the section on extensions? An extension is our second choice for fitting this border design. We subtract 1½ hills and valleys (6" in length) to get the odd-number 15. And of course, this is the option we will have to choose since we're using 4" and 3" circles.

Because we're reducing 16½ hills and valleys down to 15, that means we have an extra 6" to work into the remaining 15 hills and valleys. (Remember, each hill or valley is 4", so 1½ hills/valleys equals 6".) Now we divide the 6" by 15; that equals 0.4, or almost ½". To make things easier, we'll round up and add ½" to the 12 hills and valleys in the middle (6") leaving the outer three hills and valleys at 4" each. Rounding off the numbers will make it easier to measure and mark, and ½" difference won't be noticeable. Yes, we're there! Now we can mark the quilt.

Marking Amish Curling Feathers

I recommend turning your quilt for these borders. That means you'll mark and quilt the top and bottom borders and the interior of your quilt first. Then remove the quilt, turn it 90°, and reload it. Mark and quilt the side borders.

1. Mark vertical lines on the border with chalk to measure out the spacing. For this example, the 12 middle sections measure 4½", and the three outer sections measure 4".

2. Mark a horizontal line through the middle of the border.

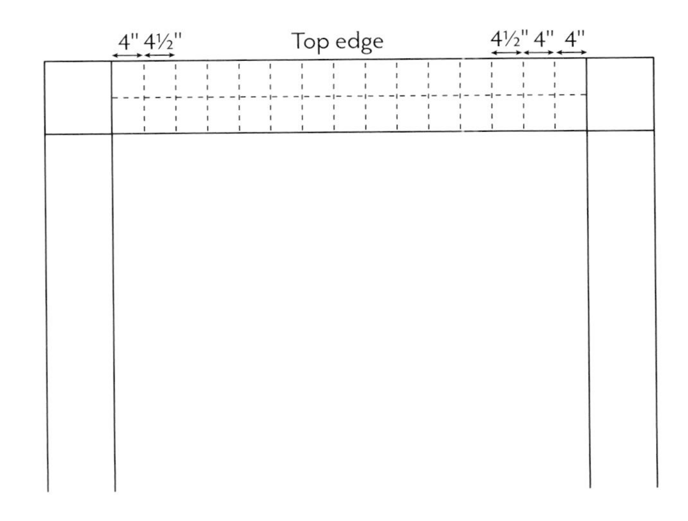

3. Using your 4" circle template, mark the curve for the main stem, stretching the apex of the center 12 hills and valleys.

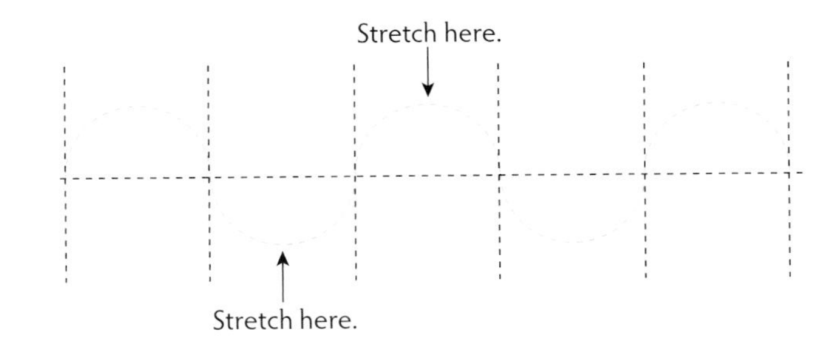

4. Mark the curling stem with a 3" circle template (shown in blue) and then mark registration lines (shown in red). The angled registration line is an approximation. Draw a straight line approximately 90° to the curl to remind you not to make the feathers on the preceding stem too large. Use a toothbrush to remove the vertical registration lines to match the illustration below. Although it's not shown for clarity, you don't have to remove the horizontal line.

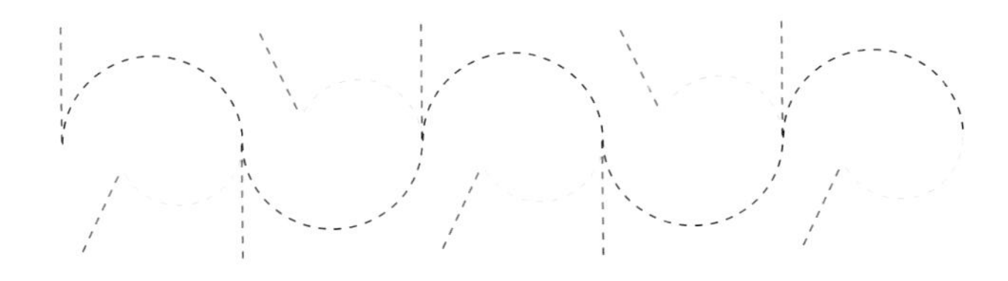

5. If you want the feathers to fill the border (extend to the edges), you're ready to stitch at this point. If you'd prefer your feathers to curve, add registration lines along the top and bottom as shown, using the same circle template as for the main stem.

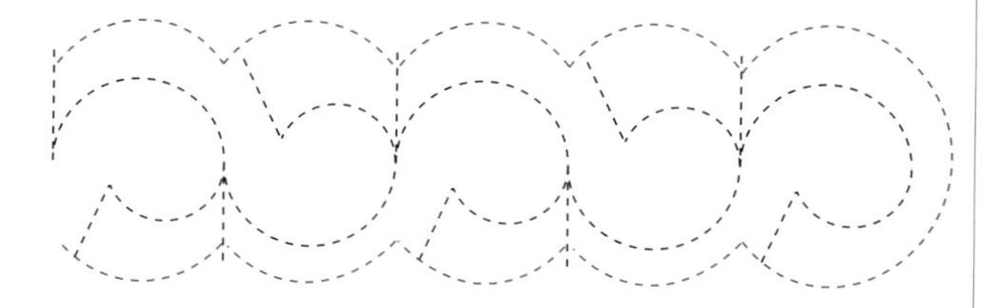

Amish Curling-Feather Thread Path

To stitch these curling feathers, use the open-quilled method described on page 25.

1. Begin at the left side of the border. Moving to the right, make the first inside curl by making a teardrop; then continue making your feathers around the inside curl.

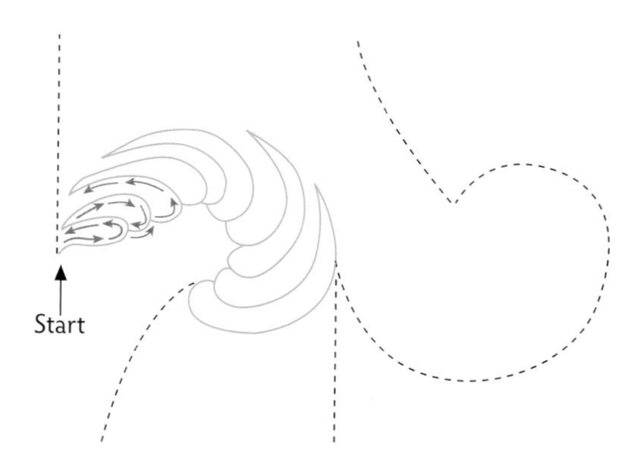

2. Close the quills by stitching left and creating the main stem.

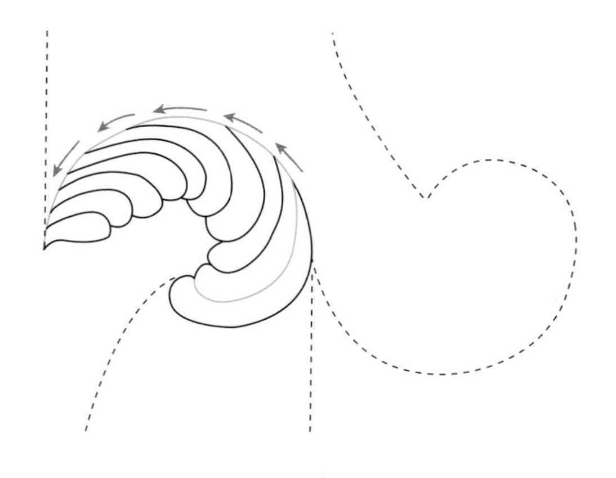

3. Make another teardrop, stitch feathers to the right around the main stem, and continue stitching to create the next inside curl.

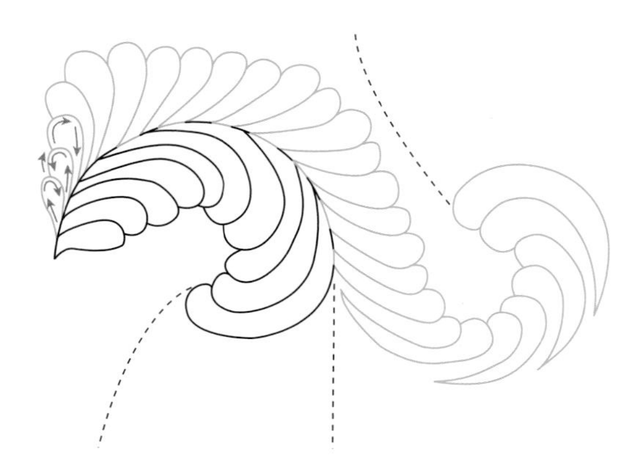

4. Travel left again, closing the quills and creating the stem.

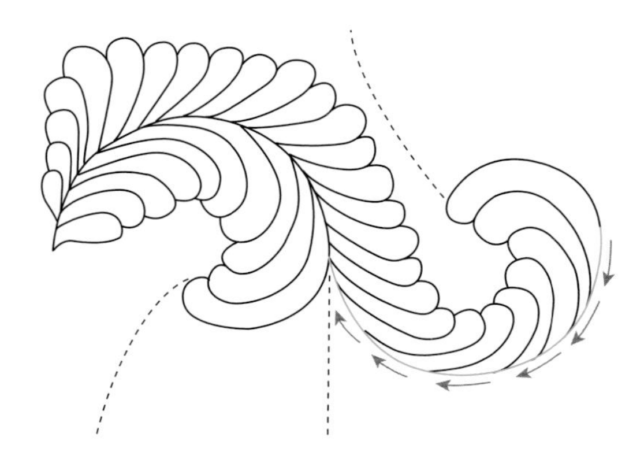

5. Create a teardrop in the *branch* and continue your feathers to the left using the last feather of the inside curl as your stem. As you get closer to the tip of your curl, make your feathers smaller and smaller and finish with a *drip* at the end.

6. Now travel to the right using the last feather of the inside curl to backtrack. Feather the main stem and continue stitching to create the next inside curl.

7. Once again travel left, closing the quills and creating the stem. At the branch make a teardrop and feather the top of the inside curl. Make the feathers smaller and smaller as you near the end and finish with a drip.

8. Repeat steps 3–7, switching to the top side and then the bottom side across the border.

"Plain Jane," pieced by Barbara Walsh and Kim Diehl. Machine quilted by Deborah Poole.

Deborah's Designs

This section contains designs that are totally my own. The Jelly-icious designs made their debut on one of my show quilts. Four Square (page 65) is a variation that I often use on quilts with open squares. Heart Strings (page 71) is my most requested design, by both clients and other long-arm quilters who would like to use the pattern. Feathered Four (page 77) was created specifically for Kim Diehl's quilt "Checkered Past" (page 77).

JELLY-ICIOUS BORDER

This is a good design to put all you've learned about registration lines, extensions, and curved crosshatching to good use. The nice thing about this border is that you don't have to worry about having an odd number of sections to turn the corner. This design is achieved by making individual arcs across the border and then the separate corner units. I suggest using this on borders that are at least 6" wide.

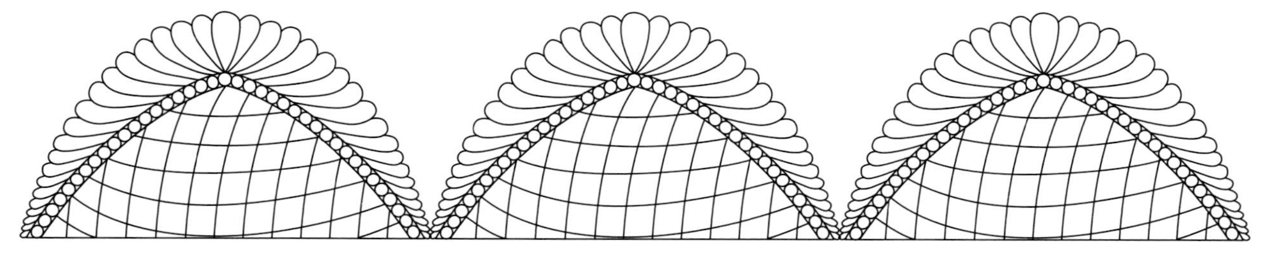

Border

Corner motif

First you'll need to decide how tall and wide your arcs will be. The width of the border will dictate the height. If the border is 6" to 8" wide, I would make the finished point of the arc about ¼" to ⅜" from the raw edge, and fill between the arcs with beadboard (page 93). In a wider border, such as a 12" border, I would make the arcs 8" to 10" high and fill with beadboard on the outside.

The length of the border will determine how many repeats of the design you'll have on each side of your quilt and will help you decide if you'll need to extend any of the arcs at the apex. After you've decided that, you can mark your registration lines. For this design I used a three-quarter ratio to decide where the cross section of the registration lines would be (A). This means that if the finished arc is 8" tall, the cross-section line will be marked at 6" (8" x .75 = 6").

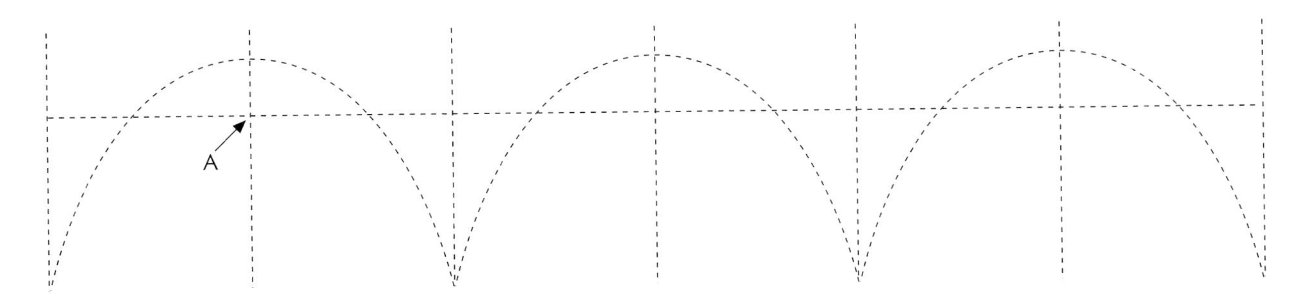

Jelly-icious border with beadboard stitching

Use the open-quilled method (page 25) and a ¼"-thick circle or oval template to create this design. If your design is 8" or larger, I recommend using the Baptist Fan arc if you have one.

1. Starting at the bottom of the left side of the arc, place your template so that it is ¼" from the bottom corner and intersection of the horizontal and vertical registration lines. Stitch to the center intersection of the registration lines (fig. 1).
2. Create a teardrop at the top of the arc, bumping up against your registration line and then feather to the left (fig. 2).
3. Stitching toward the right, use your template to stitch a ¼" channel up to the intersection of the registration lines. At the top make a little curve to the bottom of the teardrop, and then stitch the right side of the arc (fig. 3).

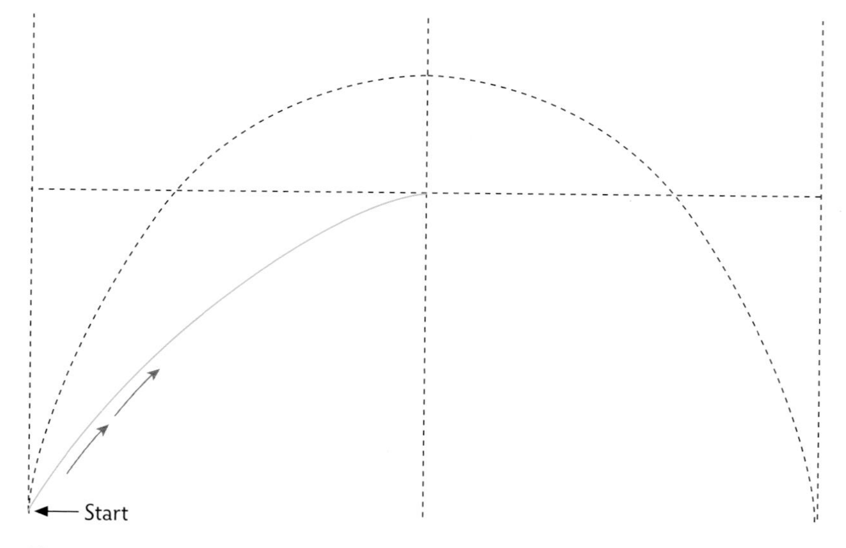

Fig. 1

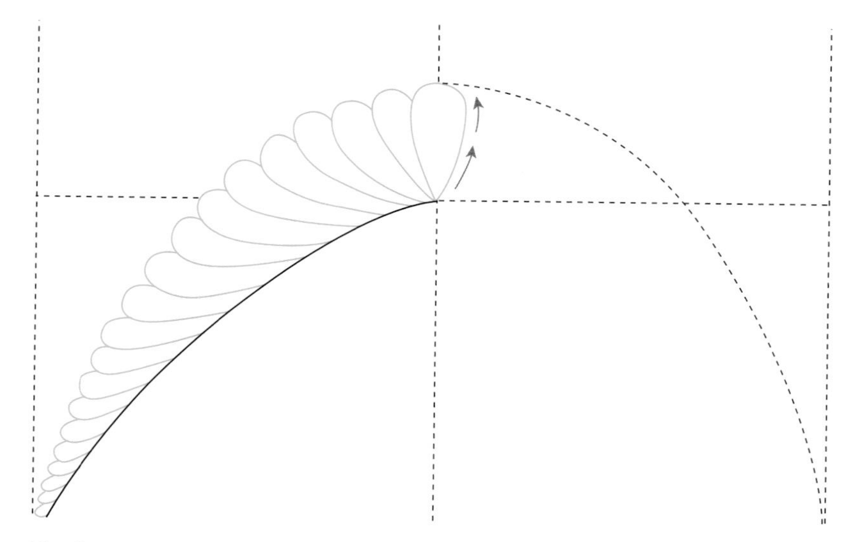

Fig. 2

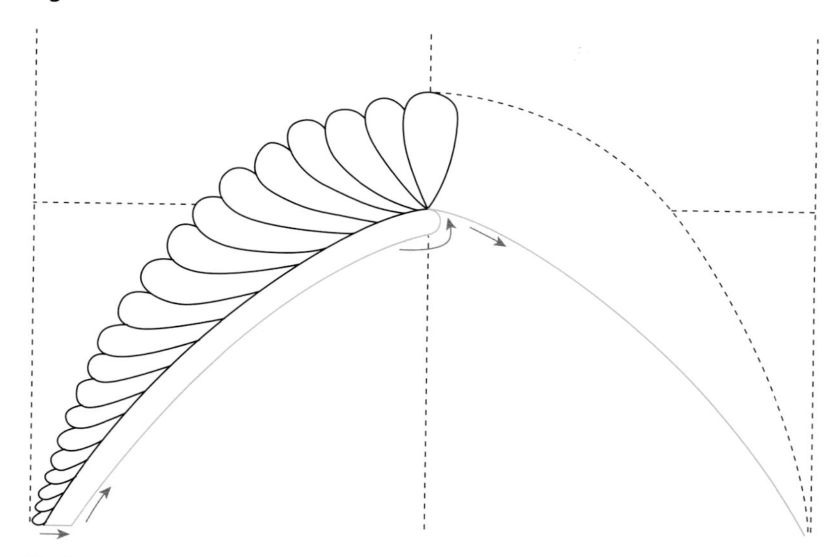

Fig. 3

4. Travel left ¼", and stitch the right side of your channel and the left side of your pearl. Then feather to the right (fig. 4).
5. Now stitch to the left, creating the first section of your curved crosshatching (CCH) using the seam on the bottom to travel in and backtracking along your channel stitches on the top. Your seam can also be used as the line to match to the line on your template to keep your CCH from going wonky. I generally stitch CCH with lines ½" apart (fig. 5).
6. Move to the top of the arc by pearling to the right and filling the left channel (fig. 6).

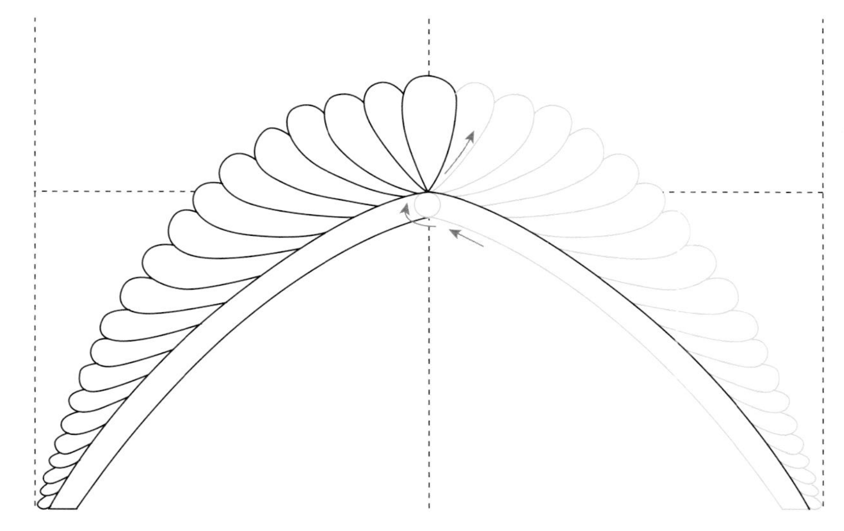

Fig. 4

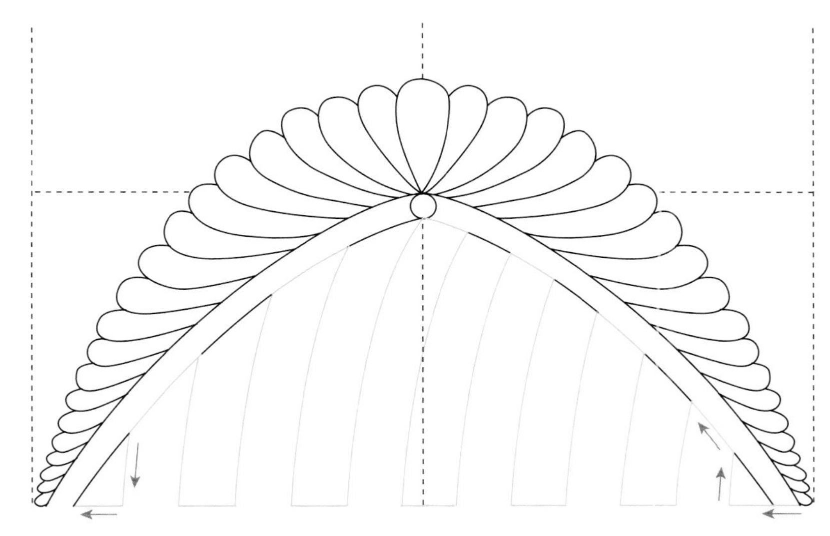

Fig. 5

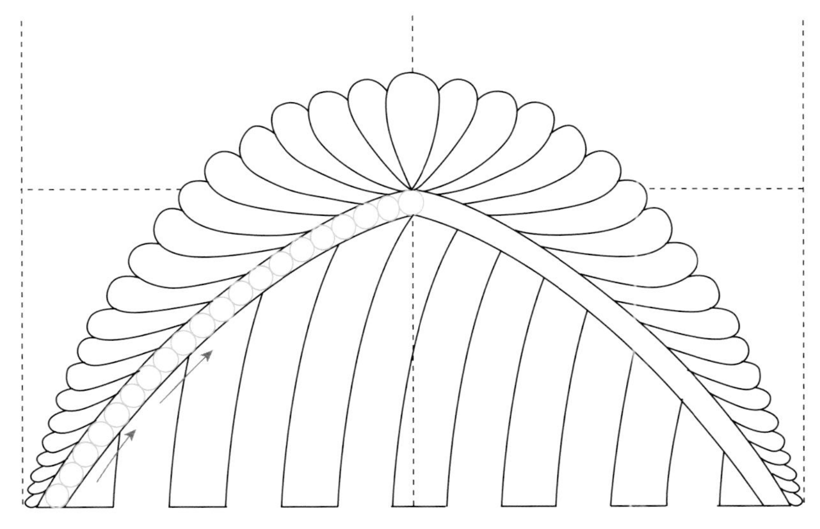

Fig. 6

7. Stitch the cross section of your CCH by traveling along the inner channel. Match your template's center line to the middle registration line (fig. 7).
8. Pearl left and to the top of your arc to finish (fig. 8). If, like me, you prefer not to break your thread to start the next motif, use backtracking over the channel stitching to travel to the bottom of the arc and begin the next motif. Plan and stitch out the corner motifs in a similar manner to the border.

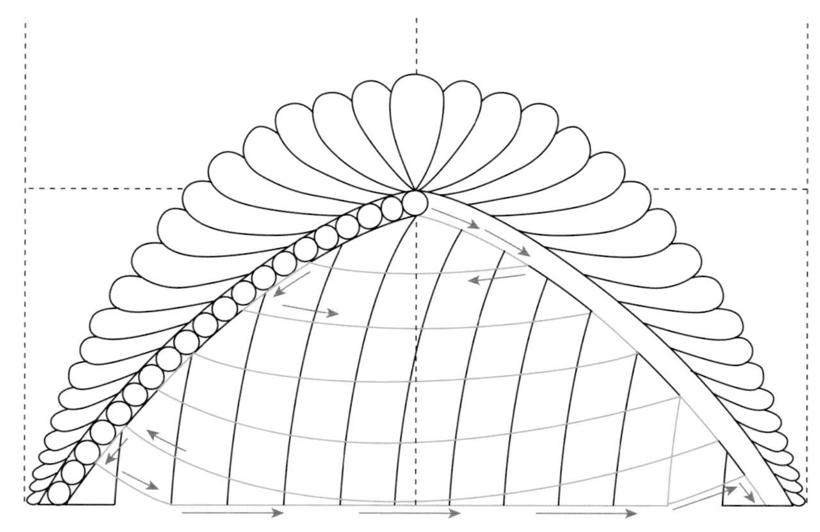

Fig. 7

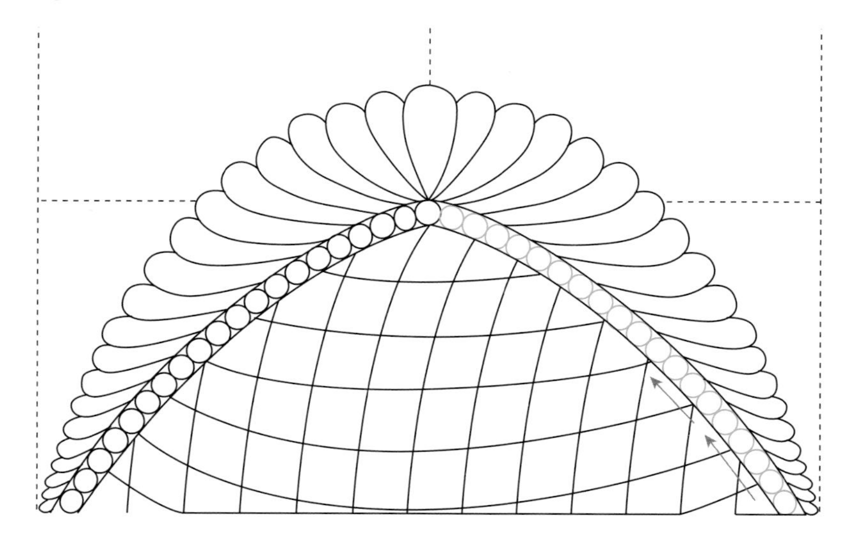

Fig. 8

JELLY-ICIOUS BLOCK

I originally designed this pattern for the setting squares of an Irish Chain quilt. It's especially nice in an Irish Chain quilt, because it's often hard to find designs that will fill the chain section next to the setting squares. The only adjustment you need to make for filling in the chain section with this design is to extend the feathers into the chain as shown in the photo.

Jelly-icious Block

Variation of quilting design for Irish Chain blocks

The registration lines for this design are really simple. Chalk an X and a plus sign through the block. Make a hash mark about one-third of the way from the corner on each diagonal chalk line (fig. 9).

Key Point~Minimize Marking

If you compare the registration lines to the close-up photo of the open space of "Jelly-icious," shown on page 59, you'll see that the hash marks would have fallen on a seam line. Whenever marking a block, look for natural breaks in the pieced top to use as registration lines. This helps keep everything uniform without the need for a lot of marking.

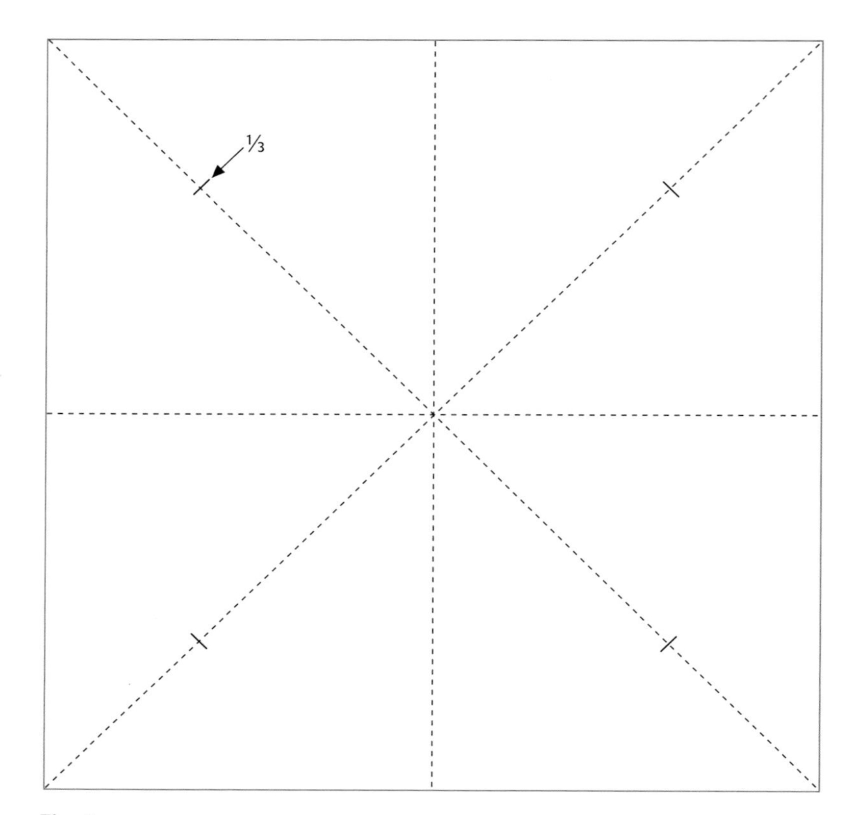

Fig. 9

Use the open-quilled method (page 25) and a ¼"-thick circle or oval template to stitch this block.

1. Start at the upper-left-corner hash mark and stitch in a clockwise pathway back to your starting point, using your template and the hash marks as guides (fig. 10).

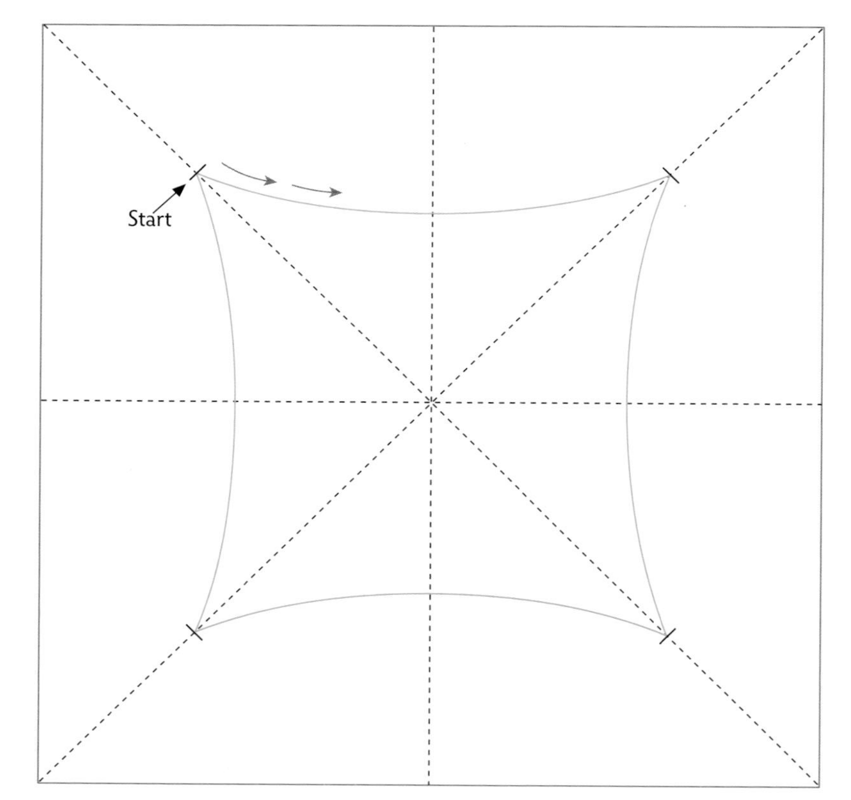

Fig. 10

2. Make three pearls, graduating in size, to travel to where you'll start your ¼"-wide inner channel. Stitch again in a clockwise pathway (fig. 11).
3. Stitch over the edges of your pearls to return to your starting point. Create a large teardrop in the upper-left corner and feather toward the left side of the teardrop, creating a swooped plume of feathers (fig. 12).

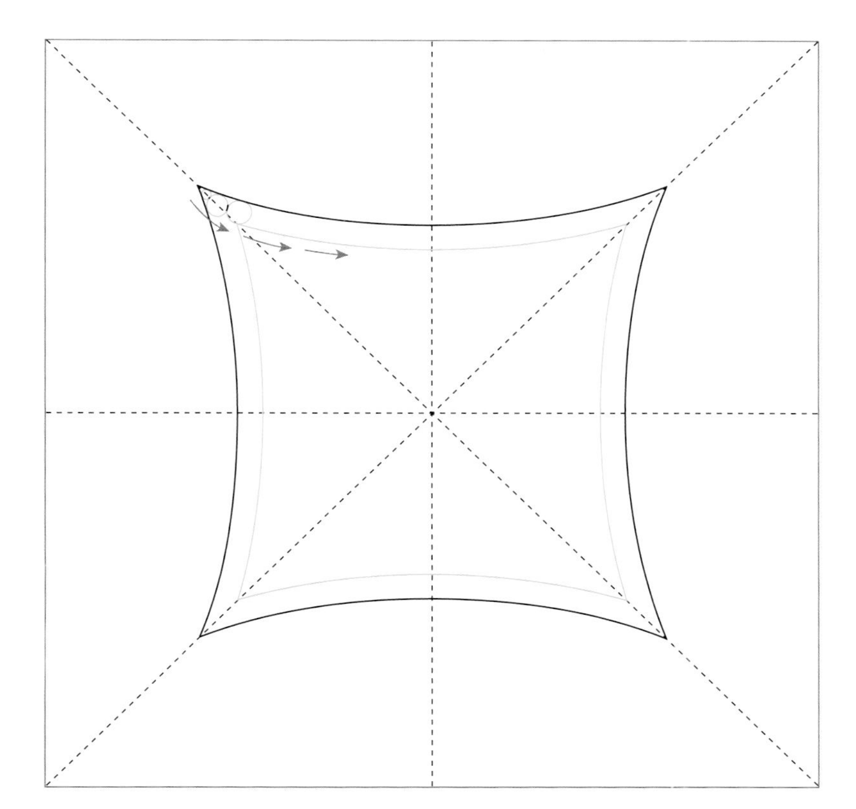

Fig. 11

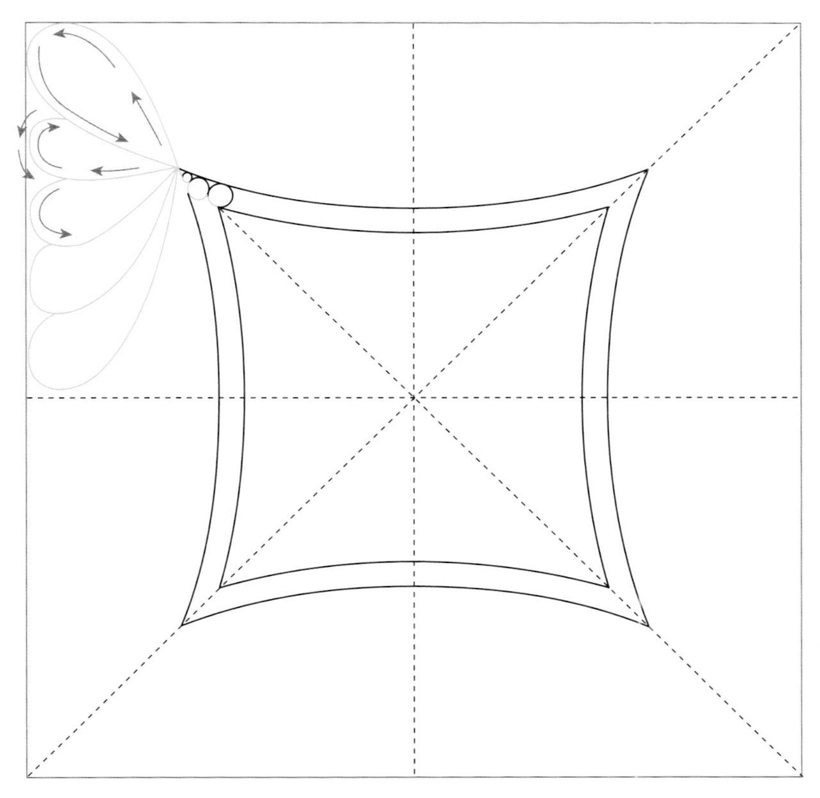

Fig. 12

4. Feather the bottom half of your large swooped feather (fig. 13).
5. Travel right along the stitching of the large swooped feather to the corner point. Stitch feathers to the right of the teardrop to create the swooped feather group, and then feather the bottom half as you did before to fill the corner with feathers (fig. 14).

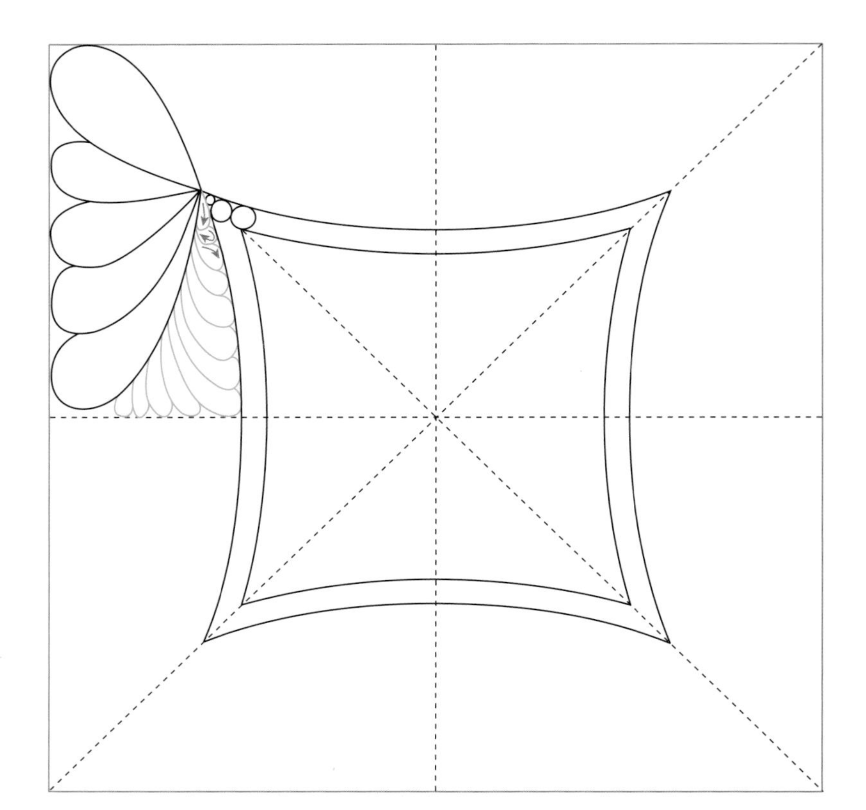

Fig. 13

Fig. 14

6. Travel left along your swooped feather and the edge of the three pearls. Transfer over the right side of the three pearls. Pearl to the right corner (fig. 15).
7. Traveling clockwise, repeat steps 3–6 in each corner (fig. 16).

Fig. 15

Fig. 16

8. Stitch CCH in one direction (fig. 17).
9. Stitch CCH perpendicular to the first stitching to create the cross section (fig. 18).

Fig. 17

Fig. 18

FOUR SQUARE

I love designs that create secondary patterns such as this. When used in setting squares, the curved channels will form a circle pattern across the quilt top. It gives a standard quilt that extra zing! You can stitch this design with or without the pearls (fig. 19).

Key Point~Identical Corners

On a design such as this, to keep that computer-generated look, I mark each corner teardrop so they are all the same size and shape.

The registration lines for this design are fairly simple. Divide the square in half vertically, horizontally, and diagonally. Then add hash marks to the diagonals first by placing a ruler from corner to corner in one quadrant in the opposite direction of the first diagonal lines. Make a hash mark across the diagonal. Then make a second hash mark halfway between that point and the outer corner. Do this in each quadrant and create a slight arc between the inner hash marks (fig. 20). This will be the registration line your inner feathers will bump up against.

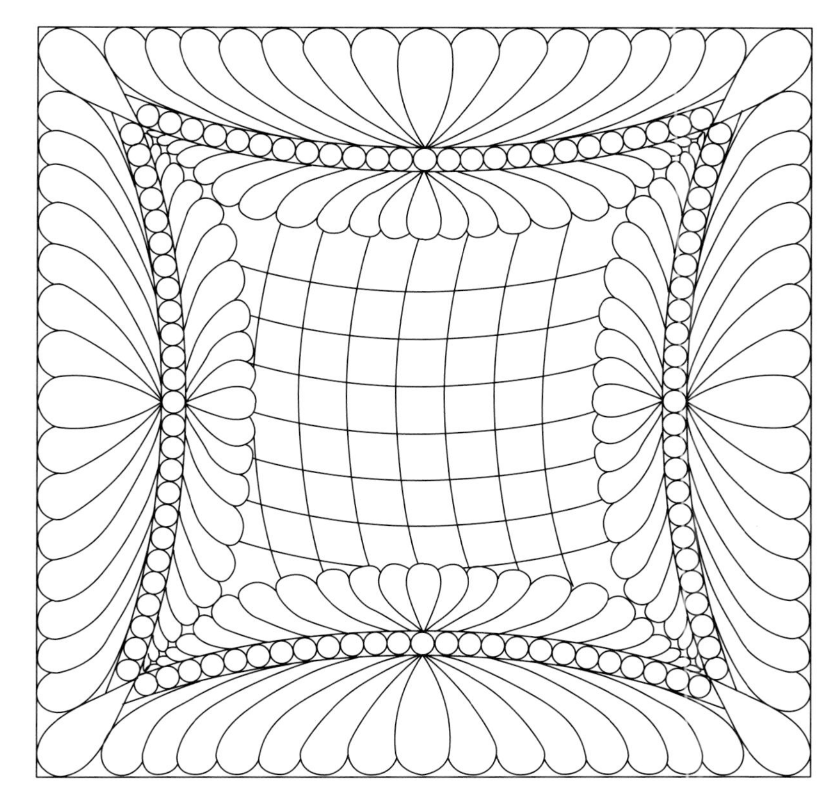

Fig. 19

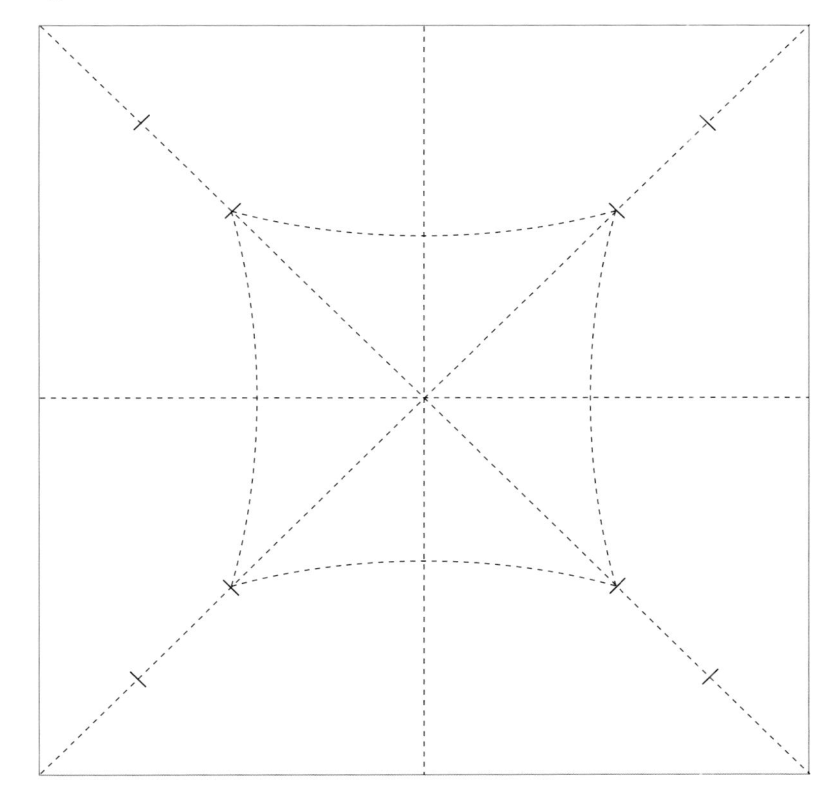

Fig. 20

Use the open-quilled method (page 25) and a ¼"-thick circle or oval template to stitch this pattern.

1. Beginning at the upper-left hash mark and traveling in a clockwise direction, stitch the inner channel line and corner teardrops. Finish at your starting point (fig. 21).
2. Stitch the top outer channel line, stopping at the teardrop in the upper-right corner (fig. 22).

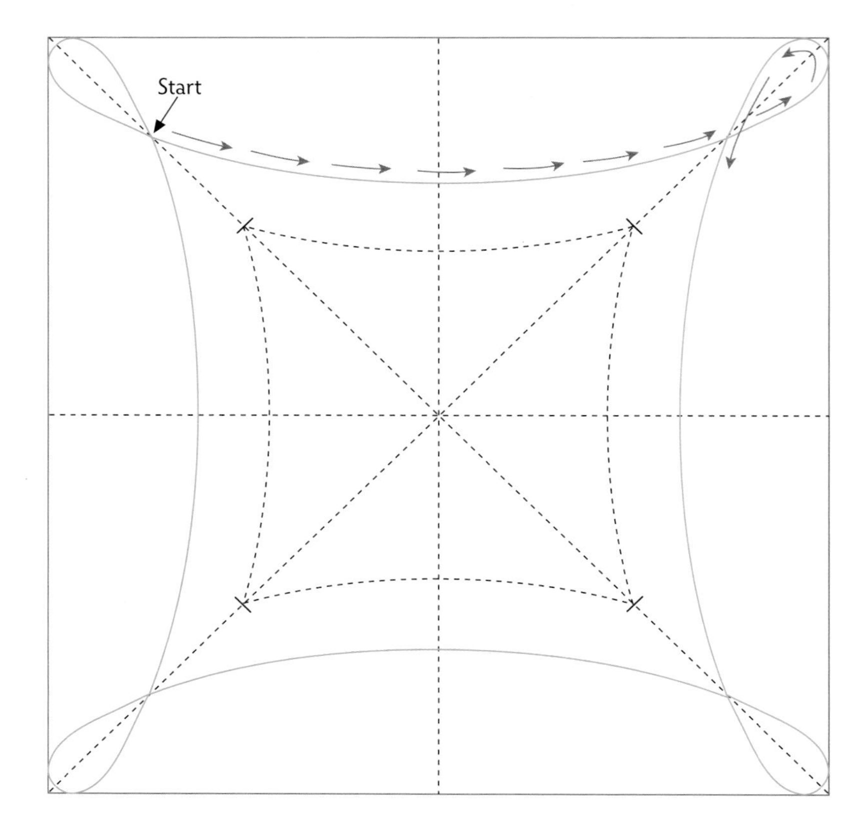

Fig. 21

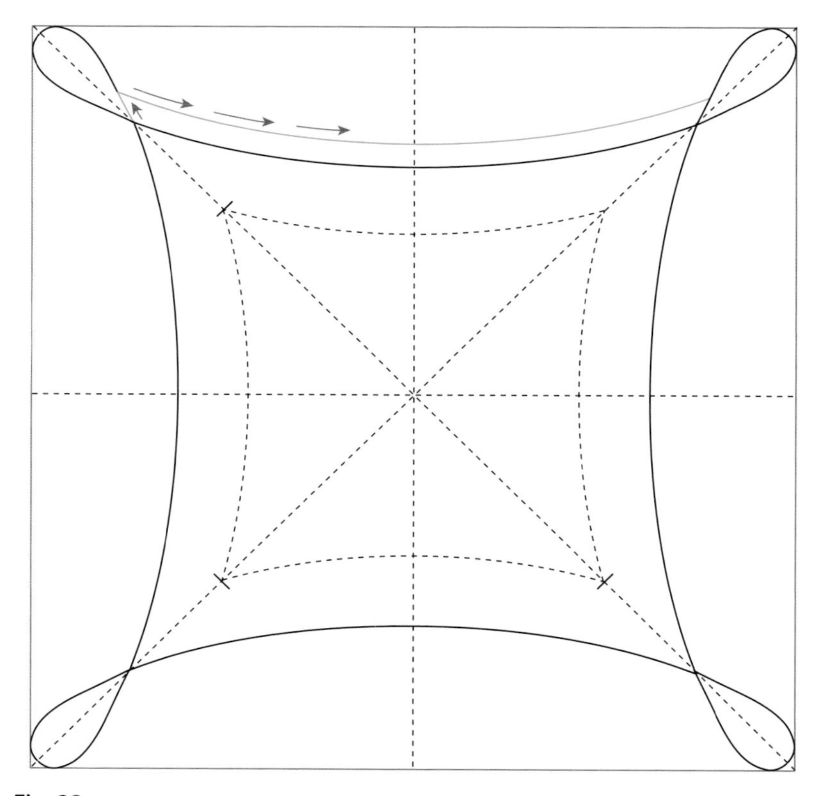

Fig. 22

3. Pearl to the left as far as the center registration line. Stitch a teardrop from the center to the top, and then feather left (fig. 23).
4. If need be, backtrack over your last feather and pearl back to the center; then feather to the right (fig. 24).

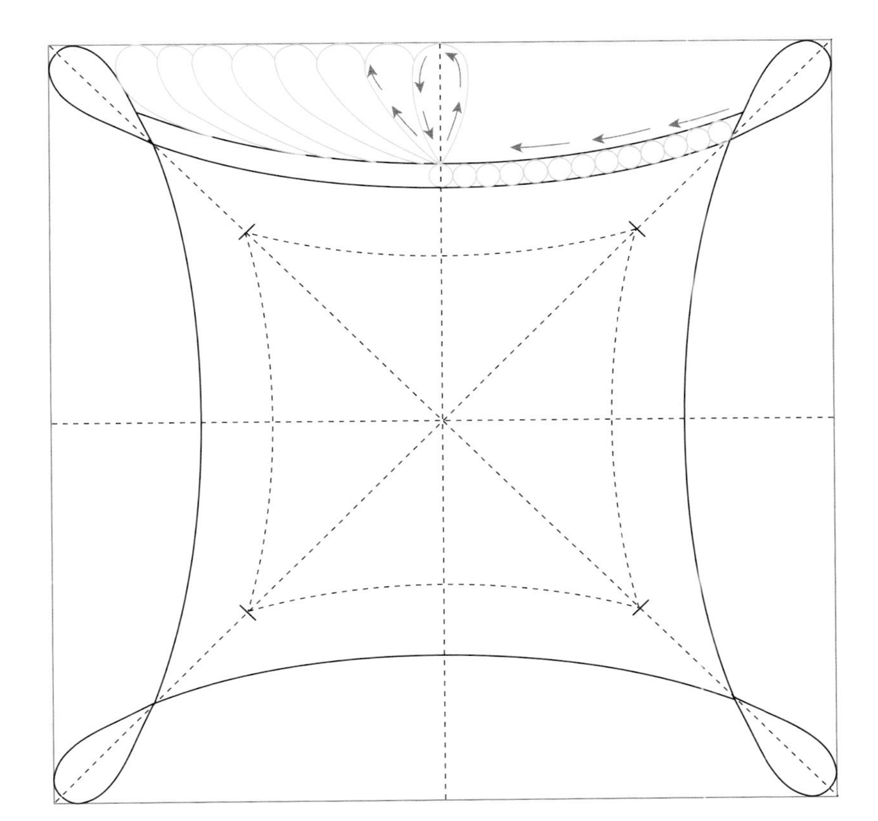
Fig. 23

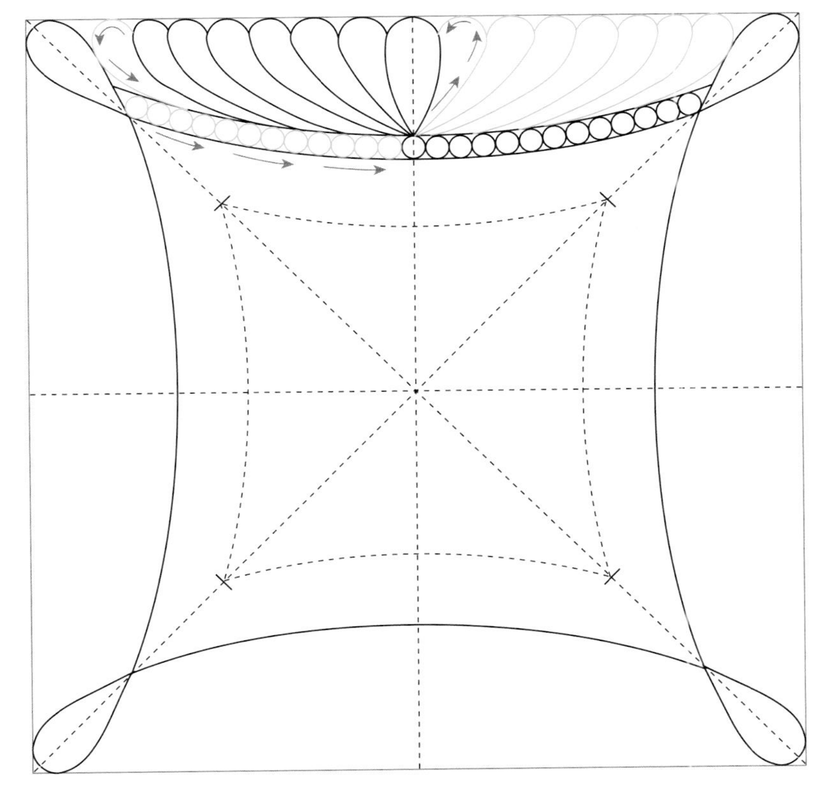
Fig. 24

5. Backtrack along your inner channel line to the center, make a teardrop, bumping up against your registration lines below, and feather left, decreasing the size of your feathers to the point (fig. 25).

Key Point~Template Assistance

When backtracking along long curves, use your ¼"-thick templates to guide your stitches for best results.

6. Backtrack along the lower channel line to the center and continue feathering to the right corner (fig. 26).

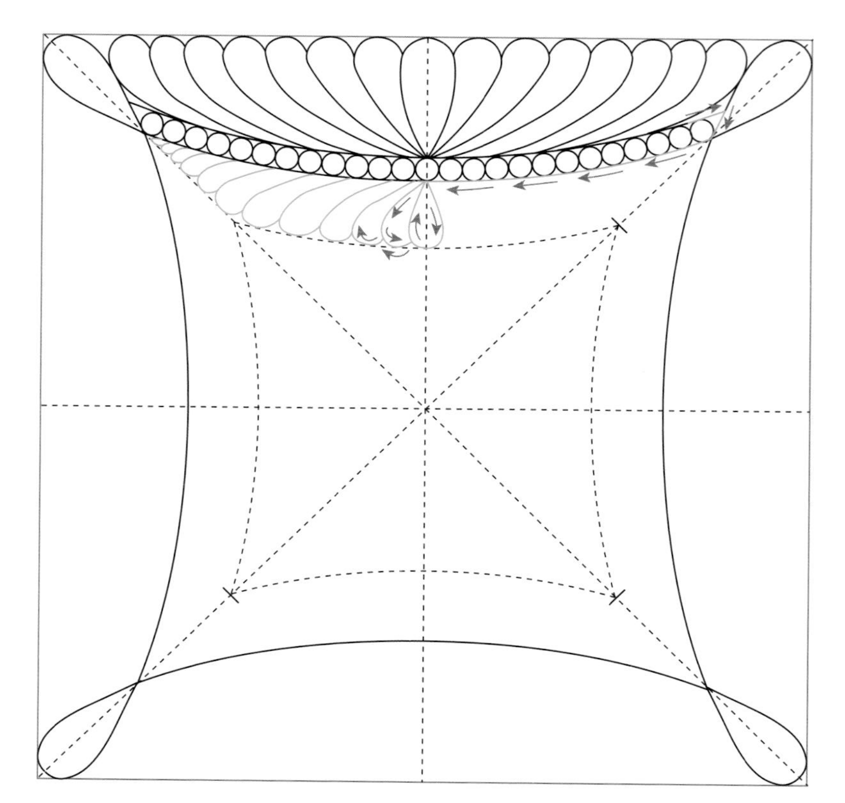

Fig. 25

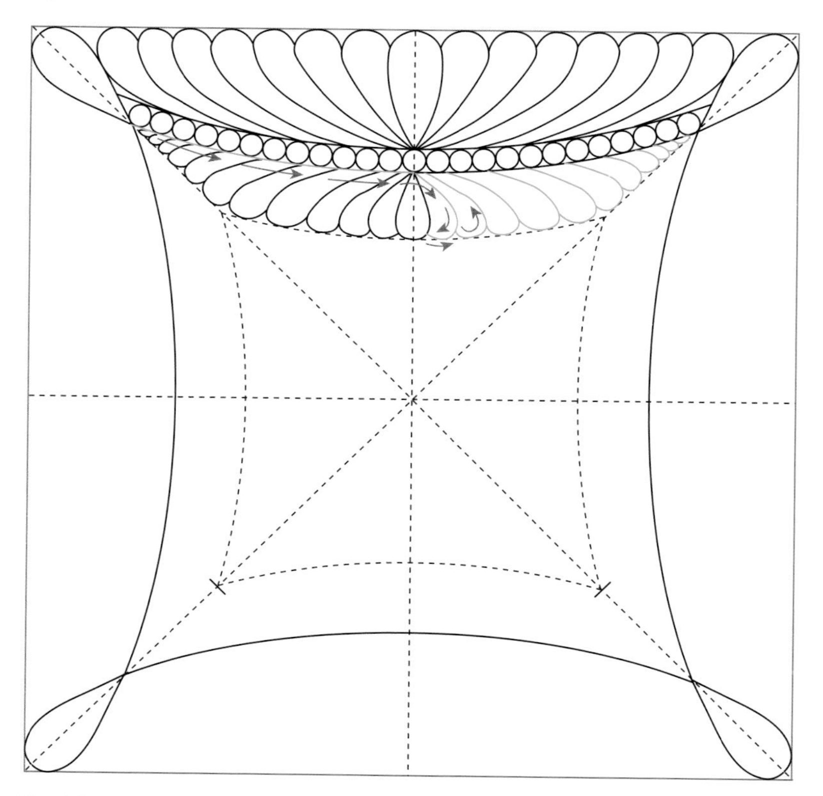

Fig. 26

7. Create the remaining three sides by repeating steps 2–6, traveling clockwise (fig. 27).
8. Travel along your feathers to the middle section of the square and stitch the downward curves of your CCH. Use the feathers to travel to the next line (fig. 28).

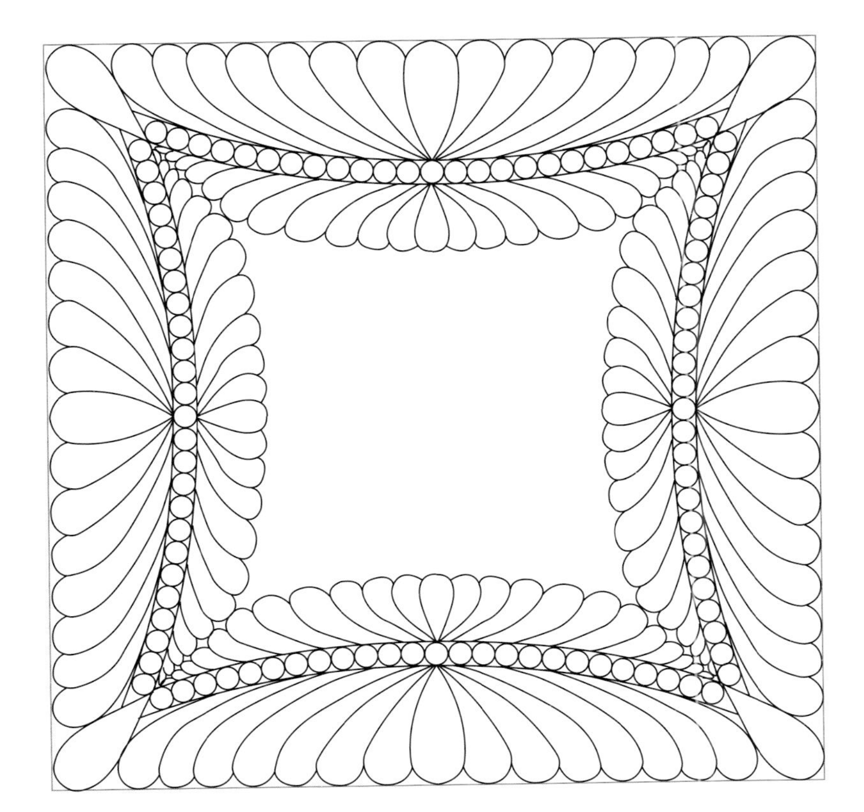

Fig. 27

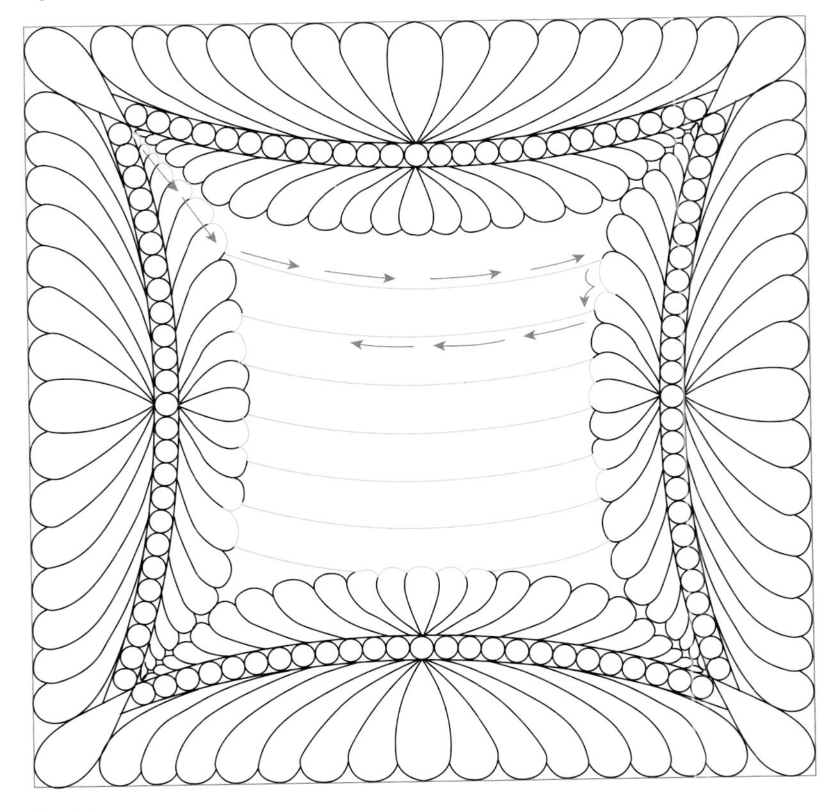

Fig. 28

9. Change directions and stitch perpendicular to the first lines to create the cross section of CCH (fig. 29).

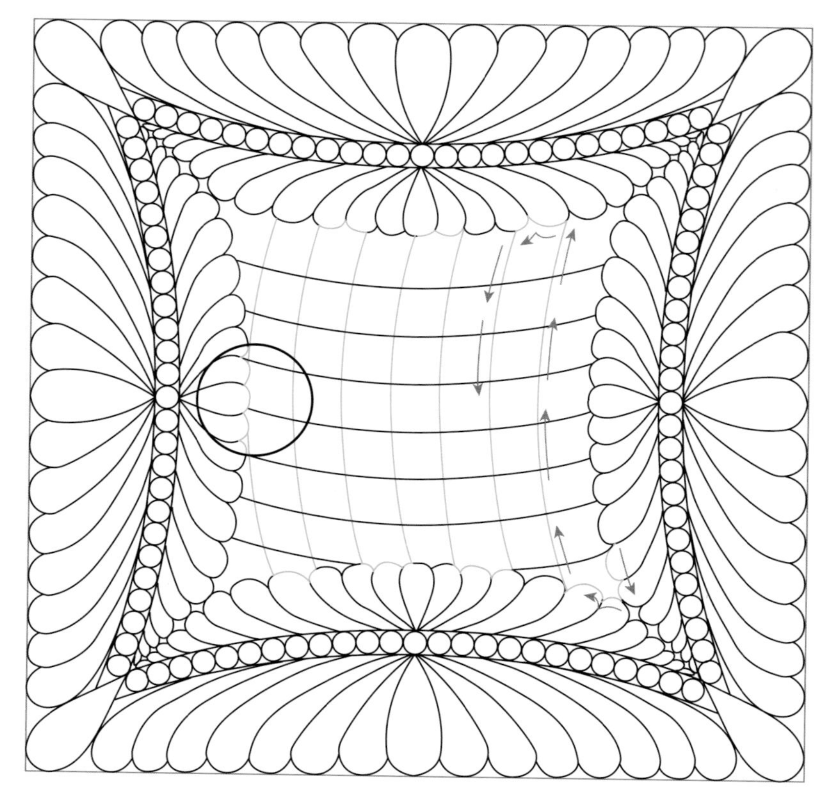

Fig. 29

HEART STRINGS

Many people ask me for this design on their quilts—even folks who aren't heart fans. Truth be told, I'm not a big heart fan myself, but I love the elegance this heart adds to borders and blocks alike. Adjust the shape of the feathers, and this makes a great design for those awkward setting triangles. Wing the feathers out, and they're a great way to fill Irish Chain setting triangles as well as a border.

Heart Strings

A variation of the design without curved crosshatching in the center

Use the open-quilled method (page 25) for this pattern. Except for the CCH, stitching this design is achieved completely freehand, without templates. You can use a circle template to assist with the curves, but I've found adding a little weight to the throat plate and slowing down makes it easier than it appears.

To mark registration lines, begin with vertical and horizontal lines at 90° angles in the center of the space. Make plastic stencils for marking the hearts. I have heart stencils in every size from 1" to 12". Mark the largest heart first, aligning the center with the vertical line. Shift the stencil up or down vertically until it's pleasing to the eye. Horizontally, the hearts may or may not be centered. Trace two smaller hearts to make registration lines for the outer channel/stem and edges of the inner feathers (fig. 30).

1. Begin at the top inner point of the middle heart to stitch the main heart-shaped stem for the feathers (fig. 31).

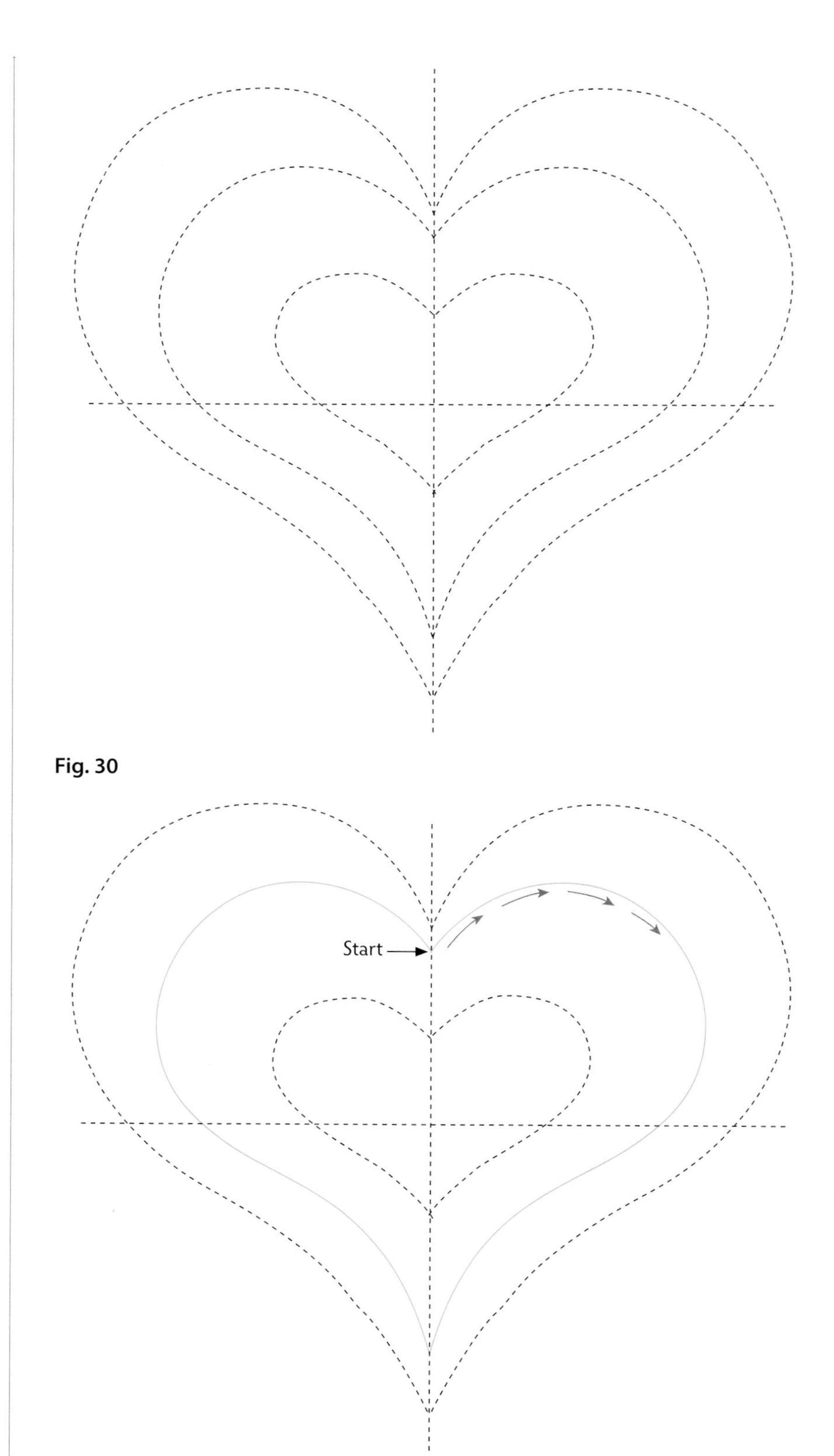

Fig. 30

Fig. 31

2. Create a half pearl on the underside of the inner point of the heart. Then stitch left to create the inner channel in the left side of the heart (A, blue). At the vertical registration line, stitch three pearls to travel to the tip of the heart (B, red). Stitch a teardrop, bumping against the outer registration line (C, green), and feather the left side of the heart (fig. 32).

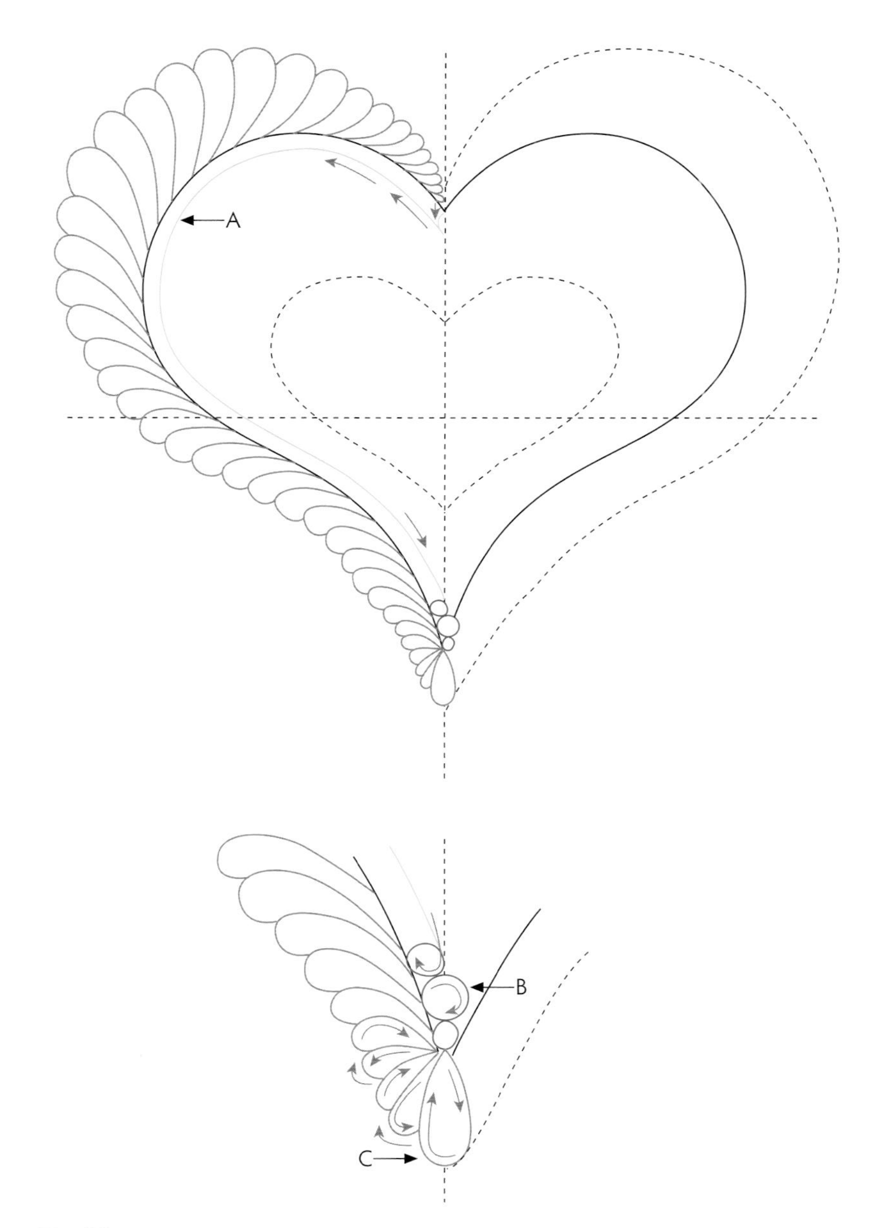

Fig. 32

3. Stitch the other side of the pearl at the inner point of the heart and stitch the right-side inner channel. At the bottom point, stitch a teardrop up toward the center and feather the inner left side of the heart (fig. 33).
4. Pearl the left channel and feather the right inner heart (fig. 34).

Fig. 33

Fig. 34

5. Pearl the right channel (A, blue) and feather the right outside of the heart (B, red) (fig. 35).
6. At this point you have two options. Stop and tie off, or backtrack along one side of the inner channel. I personally take the channel route, because as I've said before, I hate stopping and tying off. However, if you wobble into either the pearls or feathers, you'll have to stop and pick out your stitches. And I hate that even more! So for safety sake, let's stop and tie off.

   If you didn't tie off, travel along the teardrop to start your horizontal CCH (fig. 36).

Key Point~Split Your Crosshatching

Note in figure 36 that the CCH only fills the left side of the heart, leaving the right side open. Remember, traveling along the feathers to complete a direction of CCH is often necessary. That's fine if there's only one line of CCH to finish. However, if I have more than one line, as with this design, I'll stitch the full section to where it splits, and then finish one side. I'll finish the other side after my cross sections are completed. This prevents excess thread buildup along the feathers.

Fig. 35

Fig. 36

7. Stitch in the opposite direction to complete the cross sections of CCH (blue), and then complete the horizontal CCH on the other side (red) (fig. 37).

Fig. 37

Hearts and beadboard stitching make a beautiful border.

FEATHERED FOUR

Don't let this block pattern intimidate you. It's actually much easier than it looks. The design is accomplished by stitching it as two separate motifs. It's ideal for any formal quilt with big open blocks to show off the quilting.

However, it's also stunning if used over pieced blocks as in Kim Diehl's "Checkered Past," below.

Feathered Four

"Checkered Past," featured in Simple Charm *by Kim Diehl (Martingale, 2012). Pieced by Kim Diehl and Sue Makinen. Machine quilted by Deborah Poole.*

When I originally designed this block, I drew a full-sized block on graph paper (as I do with most of my designs), and then marked the registration lines on that. I then made stencils in two different sizes for the pumpkin-seed crosses, which made it quick and easy to mark each block.

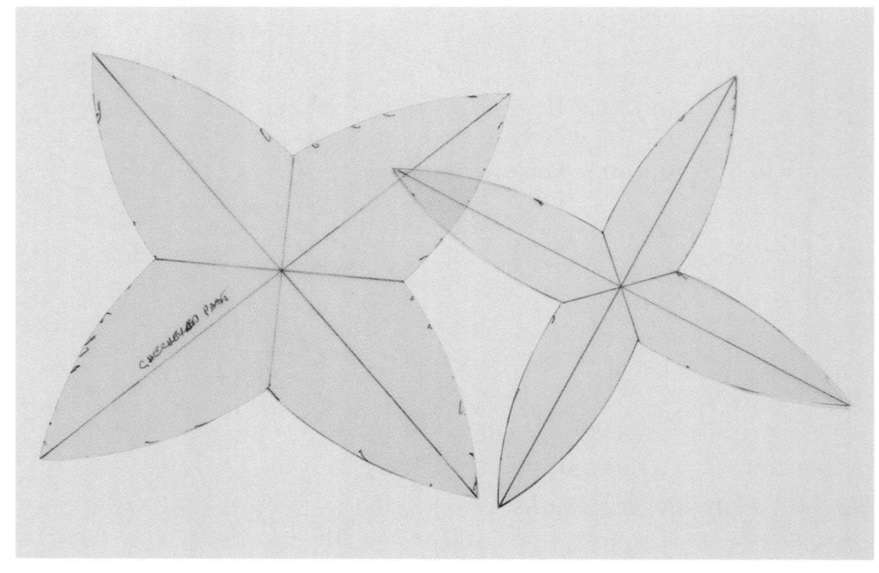

Stencils for marking registration lines of Feathered Four

Key Point~More on Hash Marks

To create hash marks without making a stencil first, divide your block into four equal quadrants. Work with one quarter of the block at a time.

1. Draw a diagonal line from corner to corner. Place a straight ruler from corner to corner in the opposite direction and mark the halfway point along the diagonal.
2. Make a second hash mark on the diagonal halfway to the corner.
3. Make a third hash mark on the diagonal halfway to the corner from the second hash mark.
4. Along two sides, make hash marks at one half and one quarter of the distance from the corner that is bisected by the diagonal line. You can use your circle or oval template to draw the curved lines, but making a stencil will help to maintain uniformity both within the block and from block to block.

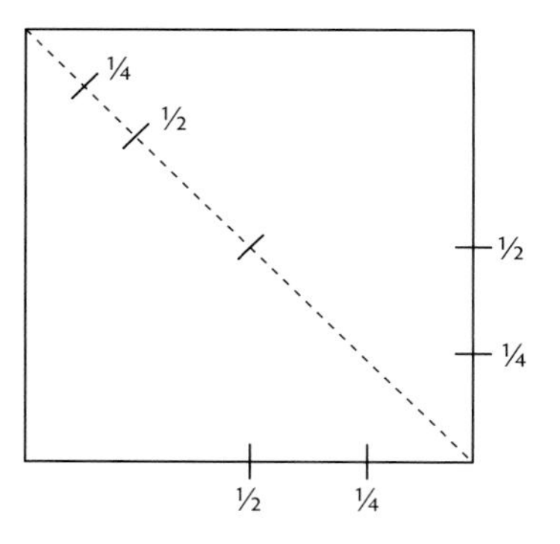

To mark the registration lines, draw the vertical, horizontal, and diagonal lines through the center of the block. Then use the stencils to draw the arcs. Make hash marks along the horizontal, vertical, and diagonal lines wherever the stencil intersects. Or, use the seam lines as I did in "Checkered Past." Also make hash marks along the diagonal, at the halfway point of the diagonal in each quadrant (fig. 38). See "More on Hash Marks" on page 78.

Use both the stemless method (page 23) and the open-quilled method (page 25) to stitch this design. You'll also use ¼"-thick circle or oval templates to make the stems and pumpkin seeds.

1. Stitch the inner motif first. Start in the center and stitch in a figure-eight style to create the center seeds and teardrops. I've found that crisscrossing at the center makes for smoother seeds, as opposed to stopping in the center each time and changing directions (fig. 39).

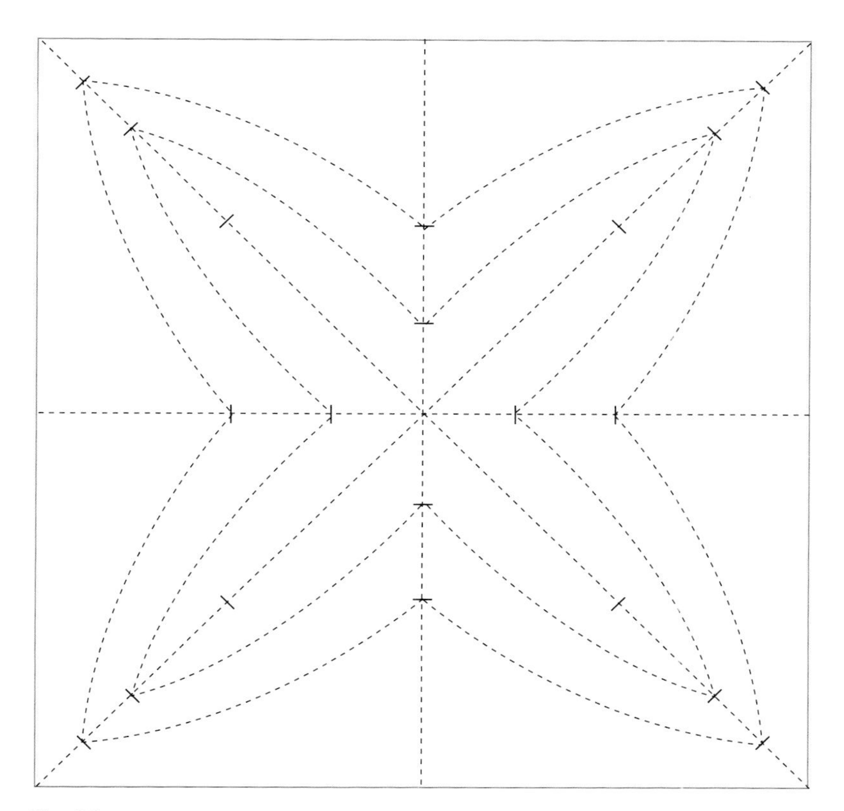

Fig. 38

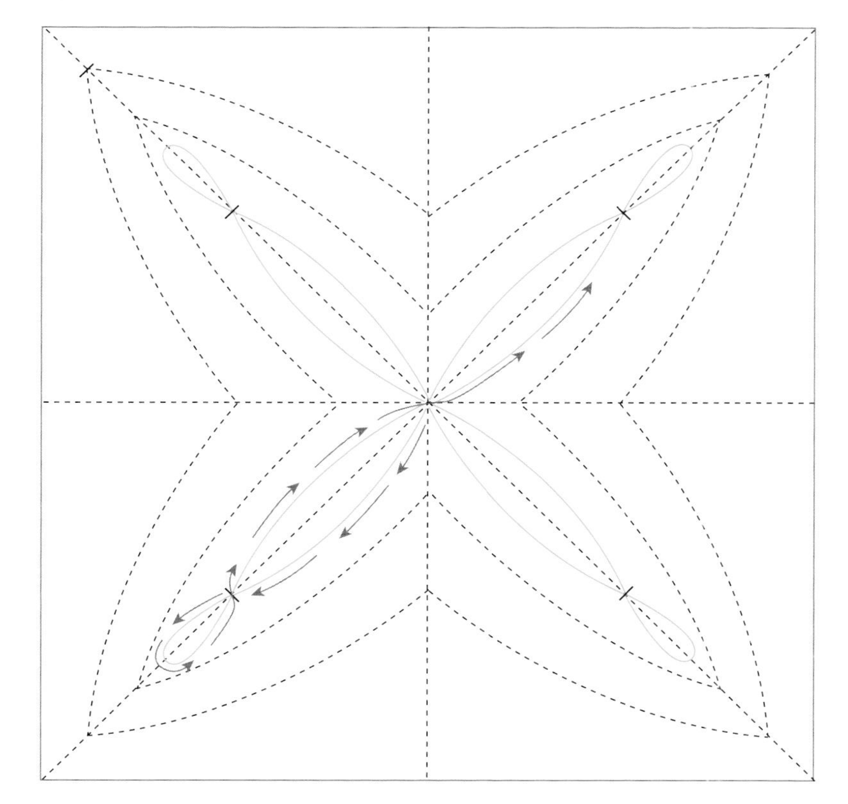

Fig. 39

2. From the center, stitch the upper-left feathered seed by first stitching a teardrop that bumps against the registration line. Then feather to the left using the open-quilled method (fig. 40).
3. Travel back to the center using the right side of the seed. Stitch a teardrop and feather the left side of the seed (fig. 41).

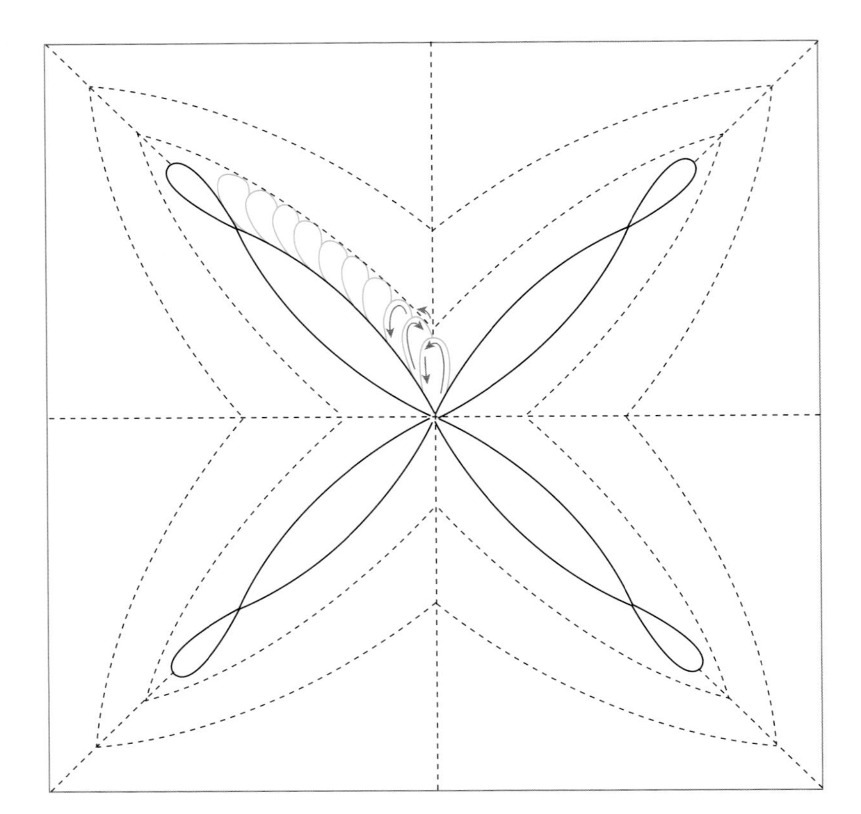

Fig. 40

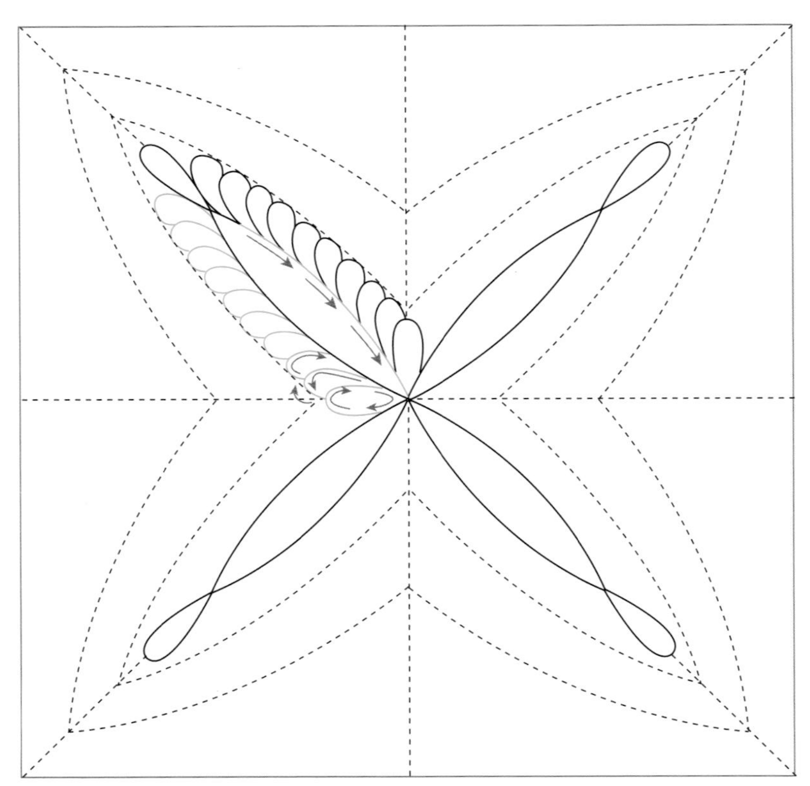

Fig. 41

4. Travel to the center using the left side of the seed and feather the left side of the upper-right seed. Travel back to the center next to the feathers you just stitched (fig. 42).
5. Repeat the process to complete the center motif. Stop and tie off (fig. 43).

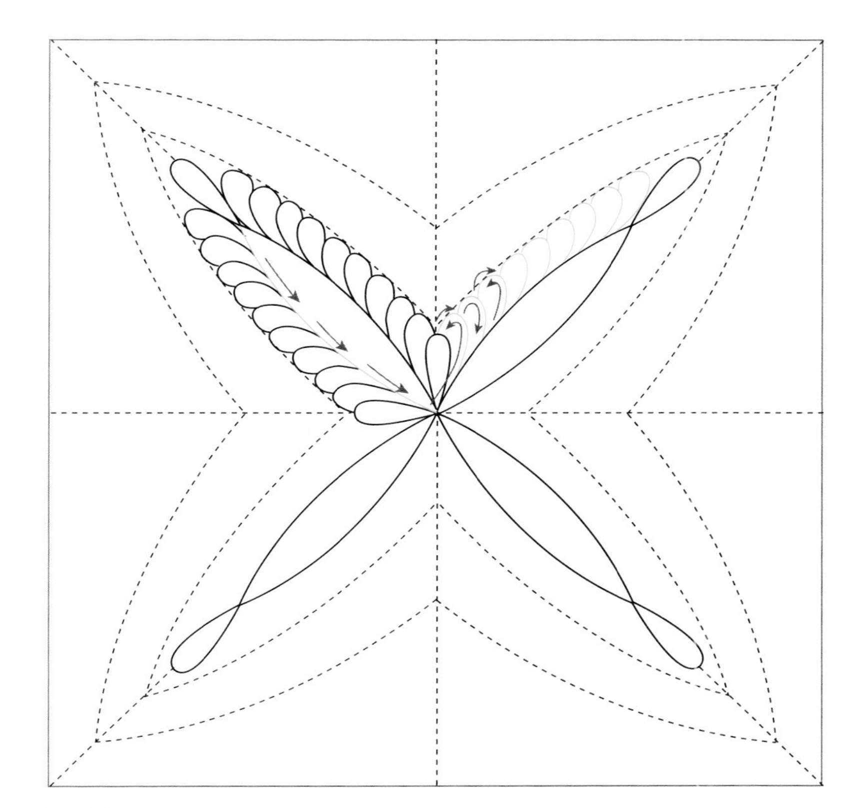

Fig. 42

Fig. 43

6. Stitch the outer motif using the stemless method. Starting at the dip or valley in the top registration line, create a teardrop figure eight, and feather counterclockwise. In the corner stitch a teardrop and then travel to the next dip, creating the stem (fig. 44).

Key Point~Feathered Perfection

If you want more uniformity in your motif, you can also mark where you want the top of each valley teardrop to be. Or do as I do and count as you stitch the feathers to make sure you stitch the same number on each side. You want three feathers, including the teardrop, to meet at that center line. Just make sure your teardrop is small enough to allow this. Try to visualize the feathers, and you will be able to visualize the size of the first teardrop.

7. Repeat step 6 working counterclockwise around the block (fig. 45).

Fig. 44

Fig. 45

8. Feather to the right on the previously stitched stem, then stitch the stem in the plume to the right, closing the quills to the bottom of the dip (fig 46). Repeat, stitching clockwise around the motif to finish (fig. 47).

Fig. 46

Fig. 47

Deborah's Favorite Fills

Many of the client quilts I work on include appliqué. I can't tell you how many hours I've spent just standing and staring at a quilt, trying to decide on a background fill for appliqué blocks. Many machine quilters get stuck in the rut of stippling. Stippling is fine and a great place to start, but if you want to take your fills to the next level, I suggest you try my favorites. They aren't hard to achieve and are very forgiving. You don't have to be exact.

Key Point~Outline Appliqués

Whenever I work with appliqué, I always stitch in the ditch around it. It helps the appliqué motif to be defined and sharp.

The other nice thing about these fills is that each one can also be used as a freehand allover design. The best way to practice these is to make them in large form on baby quilts or other utility-type quilts in lieu of a pantograph.

Key Point~Study the Small Stuff

In this section be sure to study the fillers in each sample with flower motifs to better understand what to do in small or tight areas.

LAZY LINES

Lazy lines are a great way to give a water effect to a background. They're quick and simple to apply, but add a lot of dimension. When making the lines, I like to think of the shape of a blacksmith's anvil. The flat portion of an anvil is the face, where it curves in at the throat, and the bottom is the base. Vary the length and width of each part as you go, and be sure to sometimes turn the shape upside down or on its face.

Begin and end the stitching for this design at the edge of an appliqué or in the seam of a block.

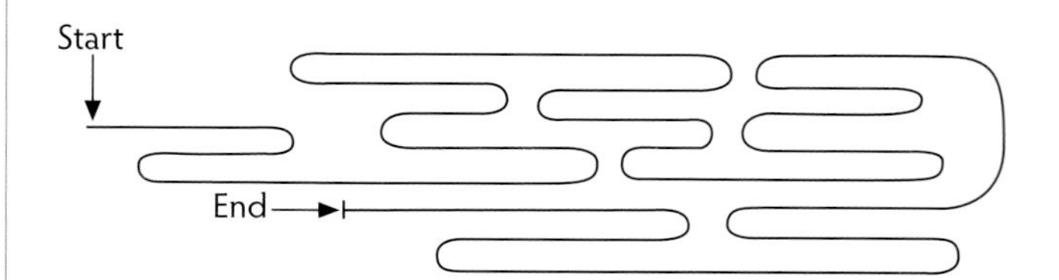

FREE-FORM ECHO

I think many people avoid echo quilting because they think the repeats need to be spaced a perfect ¼" from one another. Not true. I developed what I call "free-form echo," and it's wildly popular with my clients.

Free-form echo quilting around embroidered designs

1. Stitch a sharp echo around the appliqué (A), stitching as close to the perfect ¼" echo as possible. Then with each consecutive ring, the echoes will become less and less distinct (B). Think of throwing a pebble into a pond and the way the rings lose definition the farther out they go.

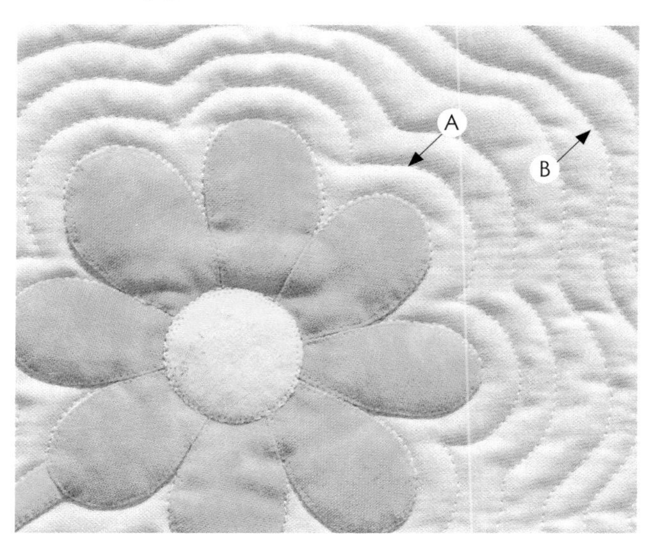

2. Fill in leftover spaces. Appliquéd blocks often have large open spaces in the corners or along the top or bottom. To add interest to these areas, I'll add other shapes to break up the echo (A). With floral appliqués, I'll often stitch butterflies, ladybugs, bees, and other motifs in those open spaces, and then echo around them.

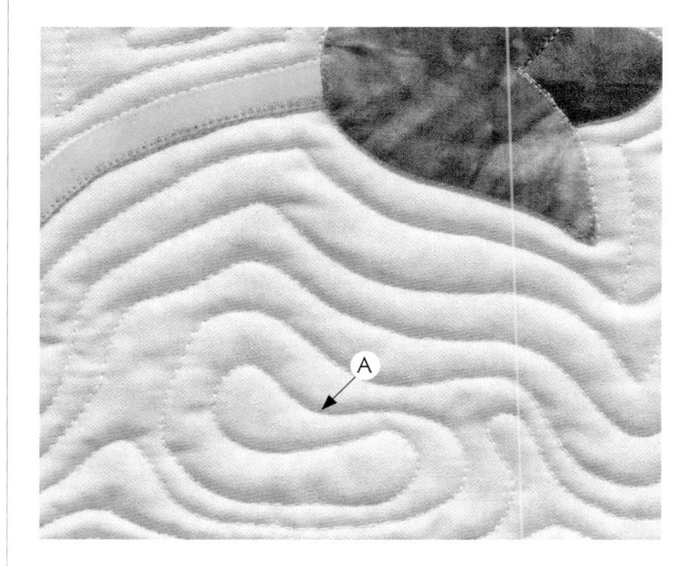

PEACOCK SHELL

I love this design. It adds great texture without difficulty.

1. Start this design by stitching a simple teardrop.

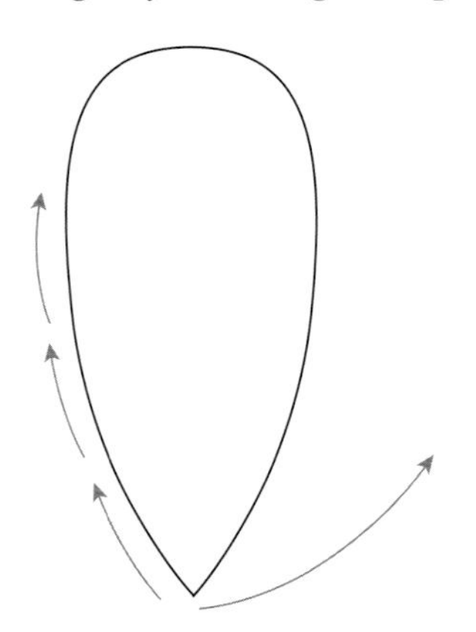

2. Reverse direction and stitch a second larger teardrop around the first.

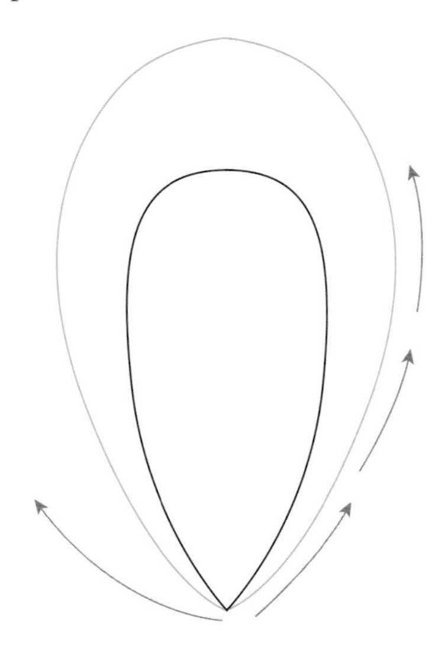

3. Reverse again and stitch a third teardrop. This process can be repeated for as many layers as you like. It can be more than three, and in tight spots you can do only one.

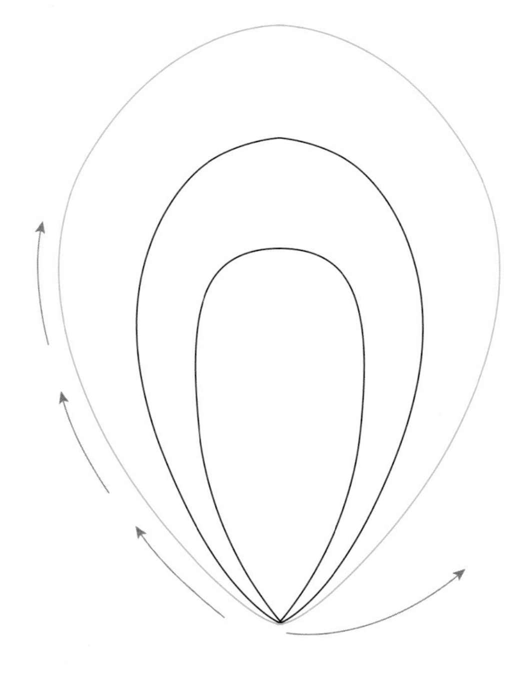

4. Start your next peacock shell from the bottom and continue stitching teardrops.

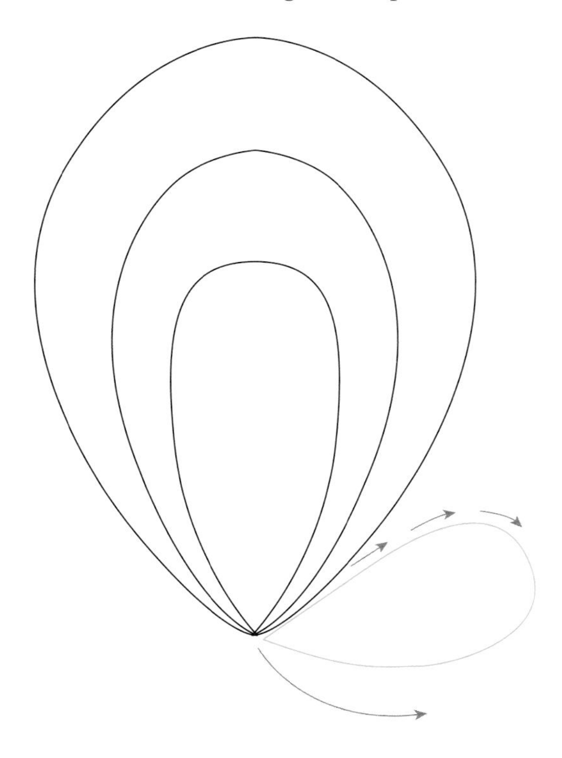

5. When you reach the edge of the block, you may end up with a lot of odd-shaped places to deal with. Don't worry about making a shell; just fill with some echo lines (A).

6. When working in and around appliqués, you can vary the size of your shells. Using both large and small shells adds interest to the texture (A).

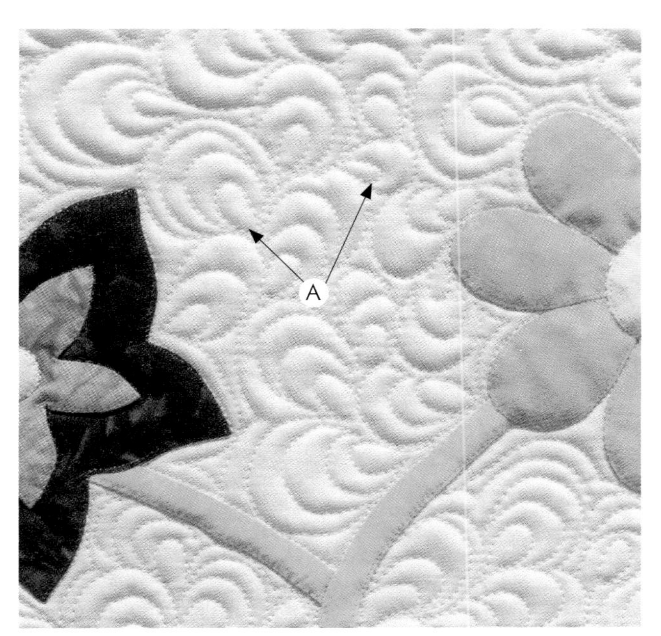

PEACOCK DAISY

This is near the top of my top-six favorite fills list. In a large scale, this is a really great allover design for an entire quilt top.

1. Start by stitching a peacock shell (page 86) with three teardrops. Then add petals to the shell. You can make them in either direction first. These petals are a cross between a feather and an arch; you don't necessarily want them to lean like feathers do.

2. Echo back. Note that you won't always echo completely around the daisy petals. Echoes are mainly used to change direction or to move to an unfilled portion of the block. Add as many or as few echoes as you like.

3. After the echo or echoes, begin stitching a new peacock daisy.

As with all fills you'll sometimes end up with oddly shaped "holes." Don't worry about making each daisy perfect. Wonky, out-of-kilter, partial flowers work just fine and are never noticed in the overall scheme of the fill.

You also don't have to worry about making a full peacock daisy. If the space is tight, just add a peacock shell or single teardrop.

MOCK BASKET WEAVE

Love, love, love this one! Did I mention I love this design? This is the only fill for which I recommend marking registration lines. It's easy enough—just decide how large you want your squares to be and chalk them in. I also make a little hash mark or arrow in or near the center of each square to keep the direction of my weave correct. I've tried to cheat many times and not chalk the hash marks. And just as many times I've had to reach for my seam ripper. Believe me, it's easier to take 30 seconds and add the hash marks than it is to rip out stitches for 30 minutes.

1. Mark a grid of squares in the size that you want to stitch. Add a small hash mark or arrow in each to keep your basket weave going in the correct direction.

2. The thread path is also easy. Here I've drawn it going straight across, but you can also stitch it on the diagonal. When you come to the appliqué, simply travel to the next square by stitching in the ditch around the shape.

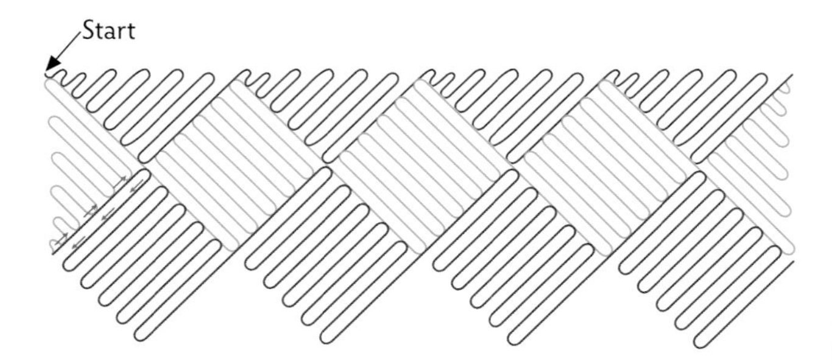

HOOKED FEATHERS

Hooked feathers make a great allover design. When making this fill, I use the long-arm feather (page 25), but you can also use the lace feather (page 26).

1. Stitch a hooked bulb. I think of it as a musical note with a wide tail. The hook can be made in either direction.

2. Feather around the hook. For me, this is where the fun comes in. I do so many formal designs, it's nice to do this one because you can really add the *funk* to the feathers.

3. Echo back and begin the next hook.

4. If you get backed into a corner, don't worry. Just make a partial echo and move to the next open area.

5. If you have an odd-shaped hole, just fill it with wonky-ness. I promise it will never look out of place.

Finishing Touches

Finishing touches are just that, the little things we quilters add to bring it all together, be it in a border or in the sashing. You can also consider pearls and channels (page 38) as finishing touches, and add them where appropriate.

PIANO KEYS

Piano keys are straight, parallel lines of quilting. They should range from ½" to 2" apart. You can make your lines farther than 2" apart, but at that point they really aren't considered piano keys. Piano keys can stand alone to make a great border, or you can add them to a feather motif. When added to the outside edge of a feathered border like Jelly-icious (page 54) or Amish Curling Feathers (page 48), they really finish the design off nicely.

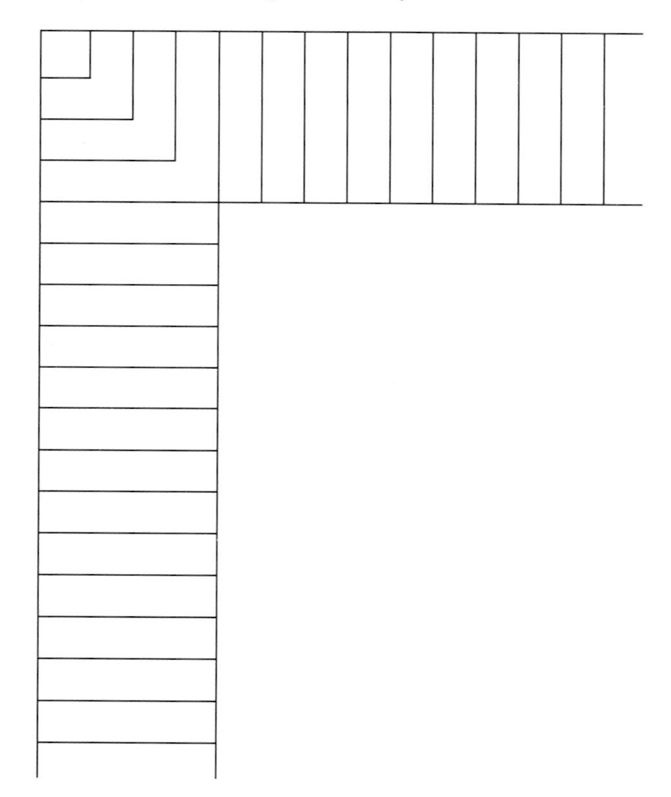

Piano keys fill a border.

When adding piano keys to a feather motif, I recommend that you don't space them any farther than 1" apart. Also, no matter how you're using them, be sure to turn the corner as shown above. Don't just run your keys off the edge as shown below.

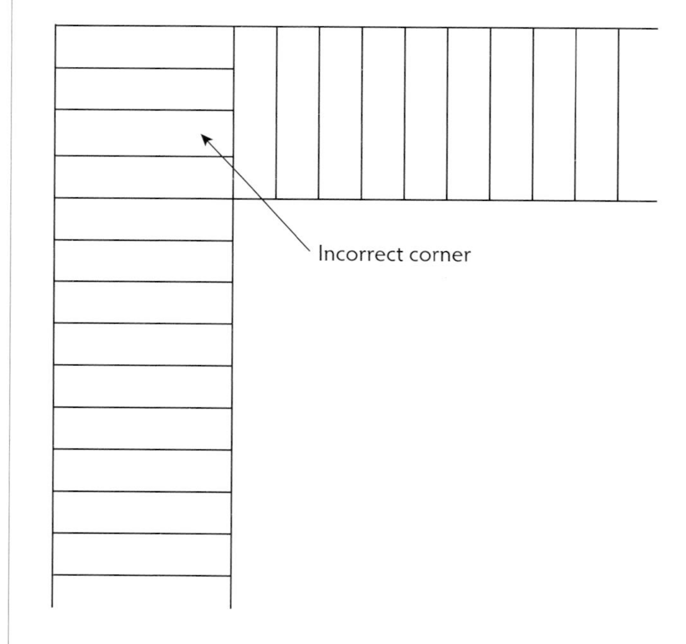

To stitch piano keys, mark the border first. Place a tick mark along one edge of the border wherever you want a line. Then simply use your ¼"-thick straight-edge ruler to guide you. Some machines come with horizontal and vertical channel locks. If yours does, it's easy to lock your machine in one direction at your tick mark and stitch. The channel locks ensure that your lines are always straight.

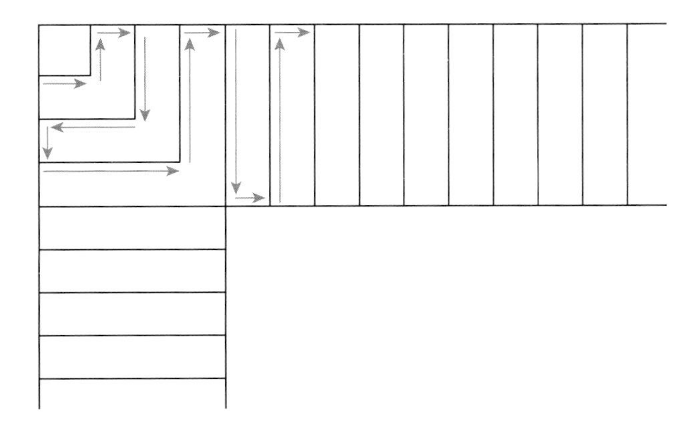

BEADBOARD

Beadboard is to piano keys what channeling is to a stem. It turns piano keys into something "wowzers." Beadboard can be used in the same way as piano keys, but sizes and spacing can be a little problematic. Beadboard is created by adding a ¼" echo to the side of a key. If you have a ½" key and you add a ¼" echo, all your distances will be ¼" apart—not a good option. Therefore, your keys should be at least ¾" wide. This will allow you to have a spacing repeat of ¼", ½", ¼", ½", and so forth.

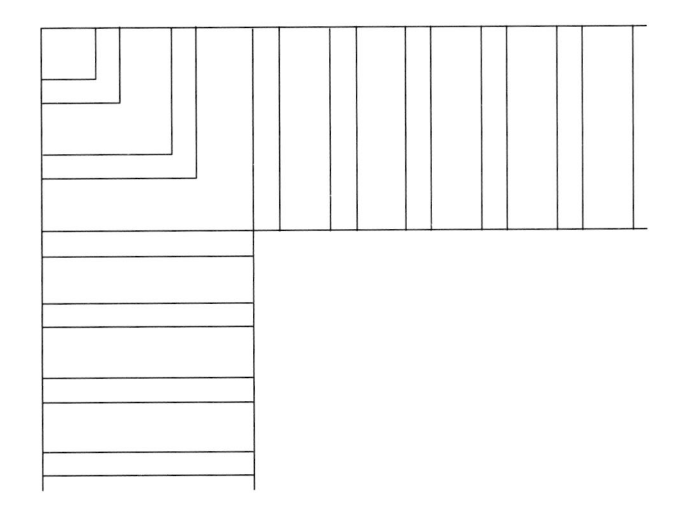

So how do you do that? Make all of the ¾"-wide keys first. This allows you to get your spacing correct, and if you need to do an extension on one end or the other, it's done without worrying about that extra ¼". You'll end up with something that looks like this.

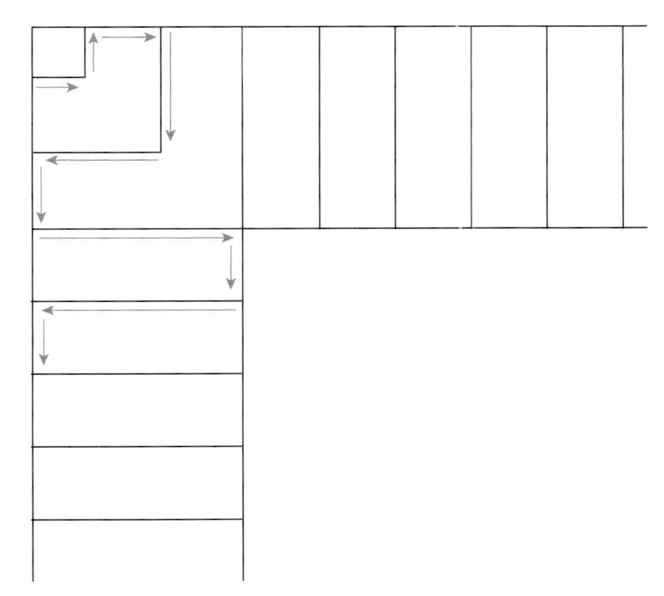

Now it's easy to go back and add your ¼" bead. Just place the edge of your ¼"-thick straight ruler on the stitching line and let your hopping foot do the spacing.

Beadboard stitching fills the space between arcs and enhances the curves of the feathers.

Key Point~Spacing Beadboard

While ¾" beadboard is impressive, it's very time consuming. The other issue is, the smaller the spacing or the closer together a piano key or beadboard design is, the more you'll notice any variations in the spacing. So for most quilts, I use 1¼" spacing. That means your spacing will be 1", ¼", 1", ¼", 1". If you need to create a couple of extensions to make them fit, it's far less noticeable.

THE INCREDIBLE EGG AND DART

The egg-and-dart design is timeless and can be seen on many antique quilts. It's a great design to stitch in sashings.

The problem with machine quilting the egg-and-dart pattern is that it's easy to let the ¼"-thick circle templates slide just a bit as you quilt. That's fine for the first pass, but if you're doing the second pass in the opposite direction (as is common), you end up with darts at an odd angle.

To alleviate this, I mark a registration line where I want the point of my dart to end up. This way, too, if you end up with a section that needs to be adjusted to fit the length of your sashing, shortening or lengthening at the apex is a breeze.

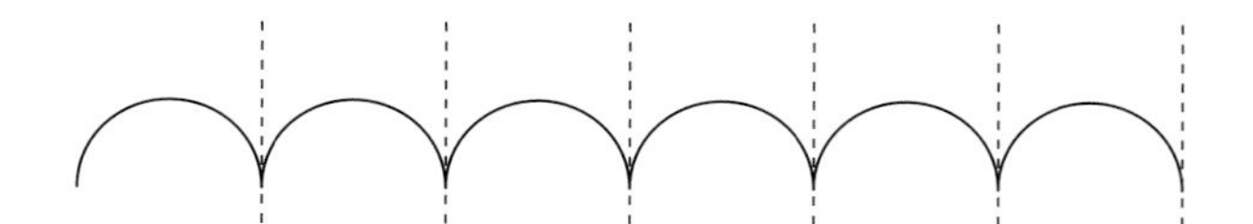

I use "egg and dart" as an umbrella phrase, encompassing a variety of designs with circles or partial circles that intersect somehow. In the quilt detail shown below, I used a single egg and dart in the sashing, but elongated it to make it fit. It created a beautiful secondary design over the entire quilt. So think out of the box and think circles. Get your architectural ruler and start playing with half-circle and circle combinations.

"Nearly Insane and Totally Nuts," pieced by Doris Coffey and quilted by Deborah Poole. Elongated egg-and-dart designs fill the sashings. See the entire quilt on page 103.

RIBBON CANDY

Ribbon candy is a pattern that weaves back and forth, resembling that old-fashioned ribbon candy we see during the holidays. I'll admit that ribbon candy needs to be practiced to get it even, but it's an awesome pattern to add texture to those skinny areas you never know how to fill.

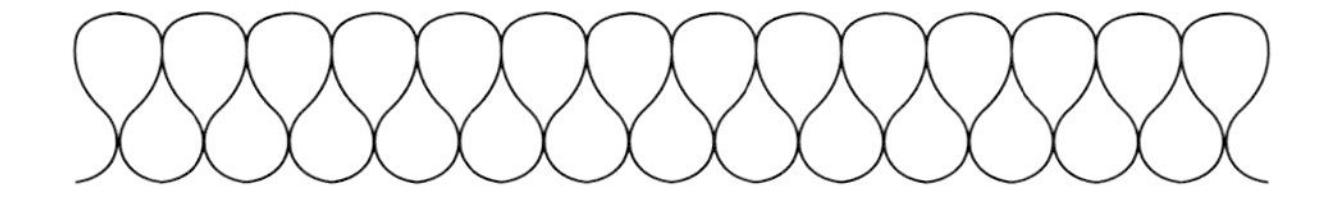

Many quiltmakers add a small windowpane either around blocks to make them all the same size, or as a tiny border around the quilt. These long, narrow spaces are usually 1" wide or smaller. While they can be left blank because of their small size, I like to add ribbon candy.

While I have stitched this design in areas as wide as 3", it's best to start out stitching it in a space that's 1" or narrower. The smaller space is more forgiving, and you don't notice any unevenness. When first practicing this design, I used heart shapes. This helped me learn to make my bulbs nest against each other properly.

Obviously, you can use hearts as your ribbon candy, but not all people like hearts, and hearts may not be the right choice for a specific quilt. Just remember that bulbs the width of a heart will be too wide, and your ribbon candy will appear flat. When you take the valley out of the heart and round it, your candy will be about three-quarters the width of a heart.

Now, as with the egg and dart, let's think outside of the box. Regular ribbon candy is great, and hearts are fun too, but when you need larger candy, what else can be done? How about double candy? I ask you, who doesn't like double the candy?

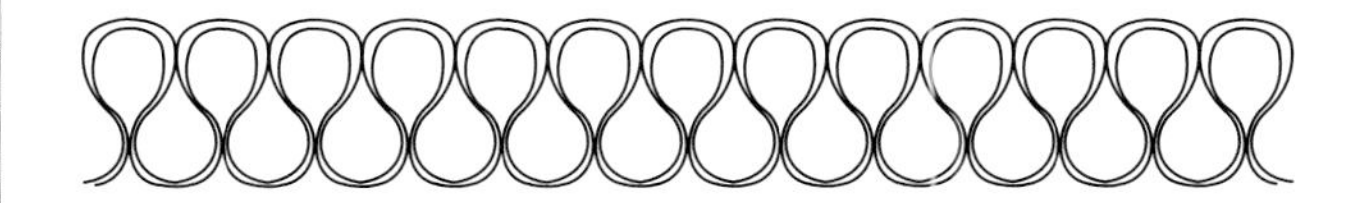

Or swirls—everyone loves swirls on their candy!

Innovative Border Design

Don't these interlocking circles make an awesome border? The first time I saw a variation of this border, I knew one day I'd have to quilt it, but I could never find anything telling me how to stitch it out. Everyone I knew who had stitched this border had done it by stitching each individual circle, and in place of crosshatching there were feathers, but again, they stopped and started for each feather section.

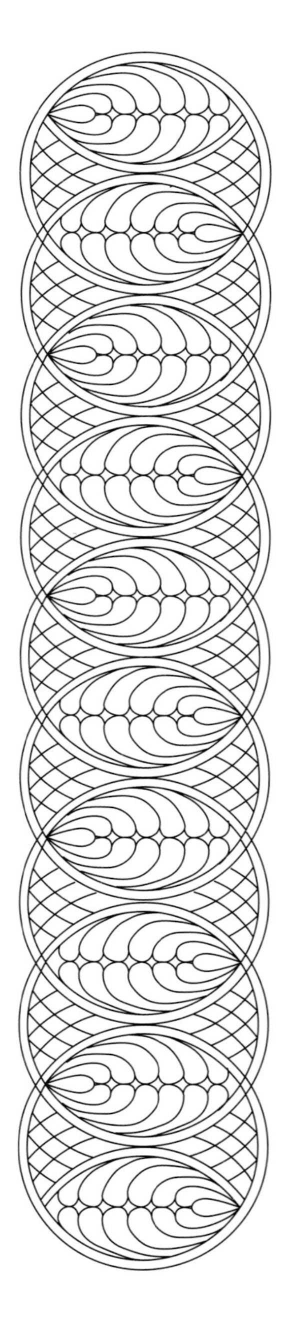

Nope, that wasn't going to be good enough for me. The thought of all those stops and starts made my stomach clench. So I sat down and made a plan. It took some time, but I finally figured out a way to stitch this border with only one start and one stop.

As with "Amish Curling Feathers" (page 48), it's best to stitch the top and bottom borders first (the borders horizontal to your belly bar and take-up bar). Then unload and reload your quilt to do the side borders after the interior of the quilt as well as the top and bottom borders are finished.

I like this design to fill the width of the border, so if the finished border is 6" wide, I want the outer circle to be as close to 6" as my circle templates will allow.

The registration lines for this border are very easy. Believe it or not, the chalk line for the middle of your border and vertical lines are the only things you need to mark. To determine placement of the vertical marks, use half the diameter of your finished circle. If your finished circle is 6", then you'll chalk the vertical lines every 3". Because we can't add extensions to circles, start marking in the center of the border and work outward in each direction. You'll adjust the size and shape of the corner units where the circles stop.

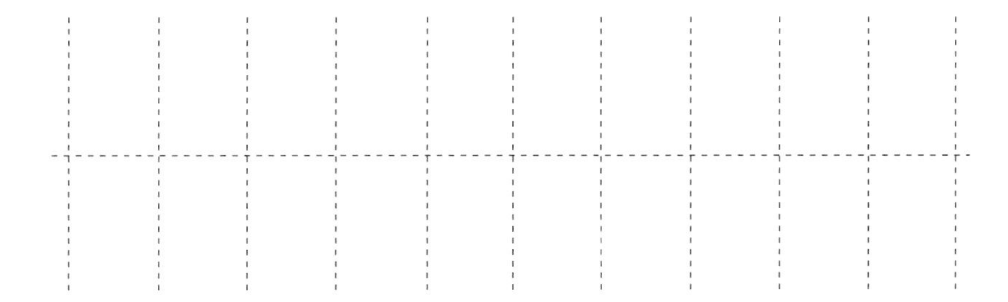

You'll need two ¼"-thick circle templates to complete this design. One needs to be ½" larger than the other in order to make the ¼" channels. For any circle size, subtract 1" from the circle diameter for your smaller circle template, and subtract ½" from the circle diameter for your larger circle template. As an example, if your finished circles are 6", you'll need 5" and 5½" circle templates.

If you don't have all of the whole and half-inch templates, you can use, for the example, 5" and 4" circle templates. This would give you a ½" channel. While I prefer ¼" channels, ½" channels look nice too. These templates would also make smaller circles—5½" diameter instead of 6"—so you would have ¼" of space on each side of the border. That is fine. Simply stitch in the ditch between the border and the quilt center. The binding will anchor the outer edge.

Interlocking circles stitched in an outer border create a fabulous finale to "Nearly Insane and Totally Nuts." See the entire quilt on page 103.

1. Using the larger of your ¼"-thick circle templates, start on the left side of your quilt by stitching a complete circle, and then weave back and forth across the middle line and complete a circle on the right side of the quilt.

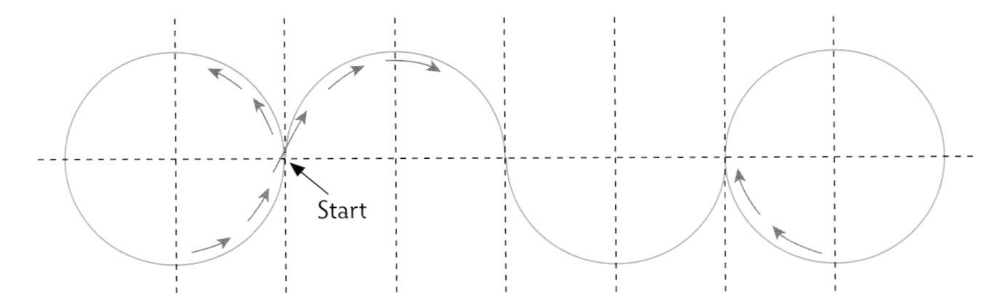

2. Move left across your quilt, repeating the weaving process to create complete circles. Backtrack along your first circle until the horizontal and vertical lines on your template match the registration lines on your quilt (halfway between the two vertical registration lines).

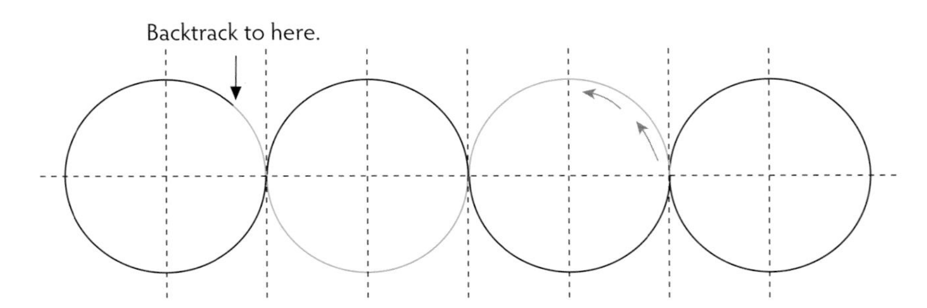

3. Stitch to the right to make half circles, ending with a complete circle along the right side.

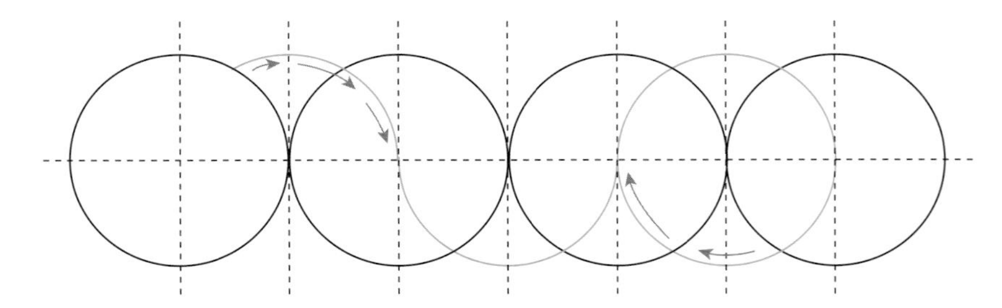

4. Stitch back to the left to complete the interlocking circles.

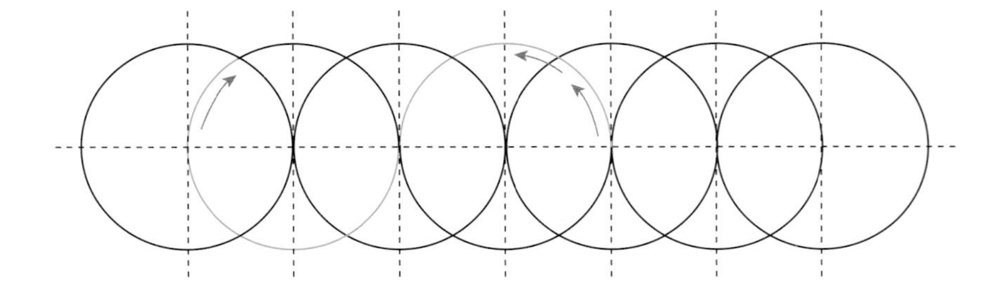

5. Using the smaller template for the inner circle, align the horizontal and vertical lines on both the circle and quilt top. Backtrack ¼" over the first circle. Traveling to the right, stitch inside the next circle until the side of your hopping foot meets the stitching along the bottom of the next circle (A). Reposition your template and repeat inside the next circle and across the quilt, creating crescent shapes.

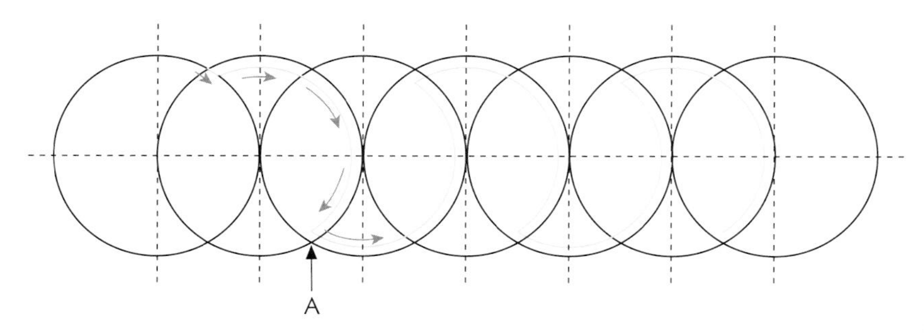

6. Stitch inside the end circle on the right to complete it, and then travel left in the same manner as in step 5. Complete the end circle on the left.

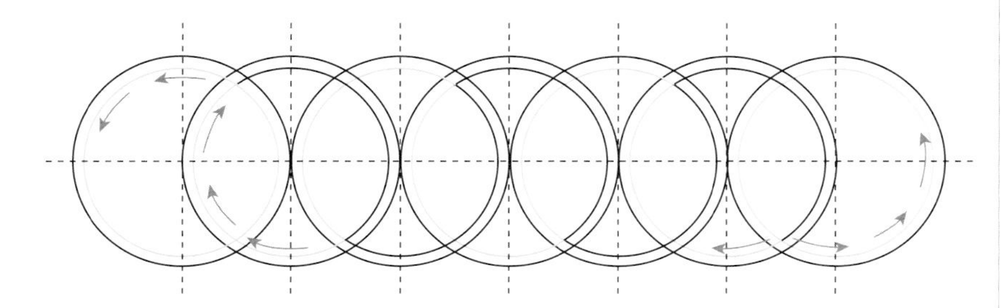

7. Stitch a teardrop and feather the left side of the pumpkin seed (A) using the line of stitching as your stem. With your larger circle template, stitch the first pass of curved crosshatching (B) (page 33). Travel on the inner channel to the base of the next pumpkin seed and feather the left side. Repeat this process across the border, first in a downward path and then in an upward path to the last circle, where you will stitch the channels to create the pumpkin seed on the right.

8. Repeat step 7 in the opposite direction. Stitch the last half plume along the left side.

9. Backtrack along the inner circle to stitch curved crosshatching in the triangular sections. Travel to the right, stitching as shown. Note how you will weave through the center of the circles to switch sides. After you finish the right side of the final feather plume, travel left along the inner channel to the next circle to begin step 10.

Refer to the diagram below for steps 10–13. Step 10 is shown in red (A), step 11 is shown in green (B), step 12 is shown in orange (C), and step 13 is shown in blue (D).

10. Travel upward by stitching along the channel to the top triangular section, and stitch the top cross section (A).

11. Travel along the inner channel of the top triangular section, and then stitch down the center channel to stitch the bottom cross section (B).

12. Referring to the longer multi-circle diagram on page 100, follow the orange lines (C) to stitch cross sections and the last half feather plume.
13. Stitch the last top cross section of the CCH, travel along the channels through the center, and stitch the last bottom cross section. These are the blue lines (D) in the longer diagram in step 9 on page 100.

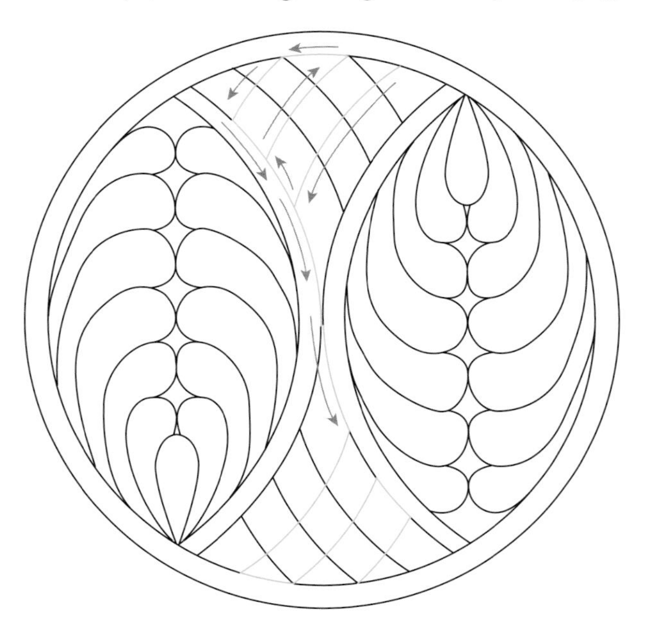

The corner sections are stitched as a separate entity from the straight borders. Stitch each corner individually.

"Nearly Insane and Totally Nuts" by Doris Coffey, 90" x 90". Machine quilted by Deborah Poole. Blocks from Nearly Insane *(Liz and Lois Publication, 2003) by Liz Lois, based on the 1870s quilt made by Salinda Rupp of Pennsylvania.*

"Wedding Quilt" by Editha Van Orden, 98" x 130".
Machine quilted by Deborah Poole. Owned by Melissa Borders.
The original quilt pattern, "Duty, Honor, Country," was designed by
Kelly Corbridge and published in McCall's Quilting *(February 2005).*

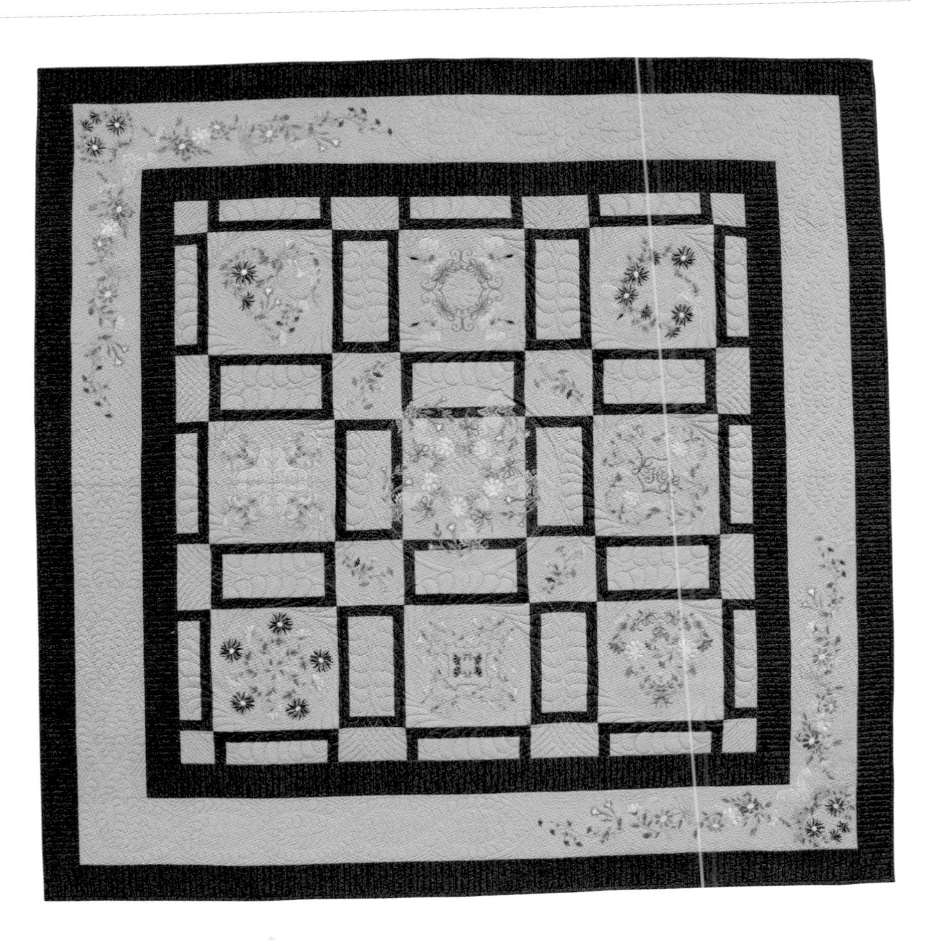

"Salmon Splendor," pieced and machine embroidered by Beverly Hindman; machine quilted by Deborah Poole; 70" x 73". Embroidered designs titled Floral Visions by Oklahoma Embroidery Supply and Design. Quilt layout design by Susan Fears.

"Oh Good Gosh!" by the late Sharon Del Pino; machine quilted by Deborah Poole; 80" x 94".

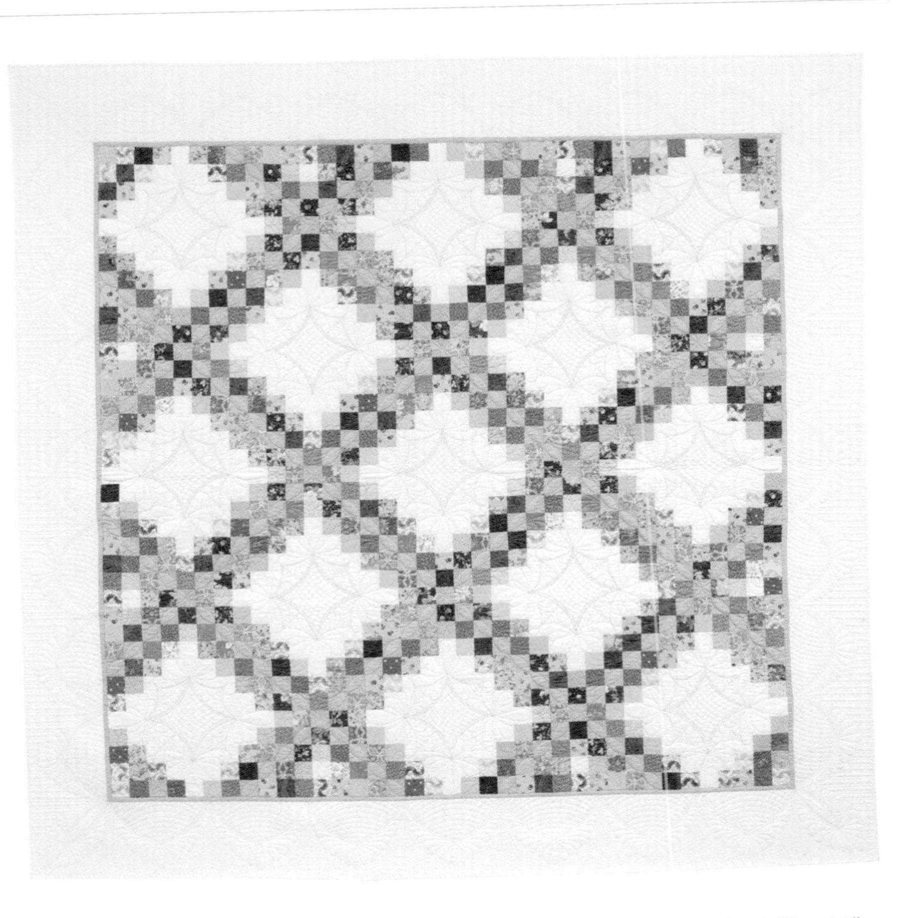

"Jelly-icious," pieced and machine quilted by Deborah Poole; 84" x 84".

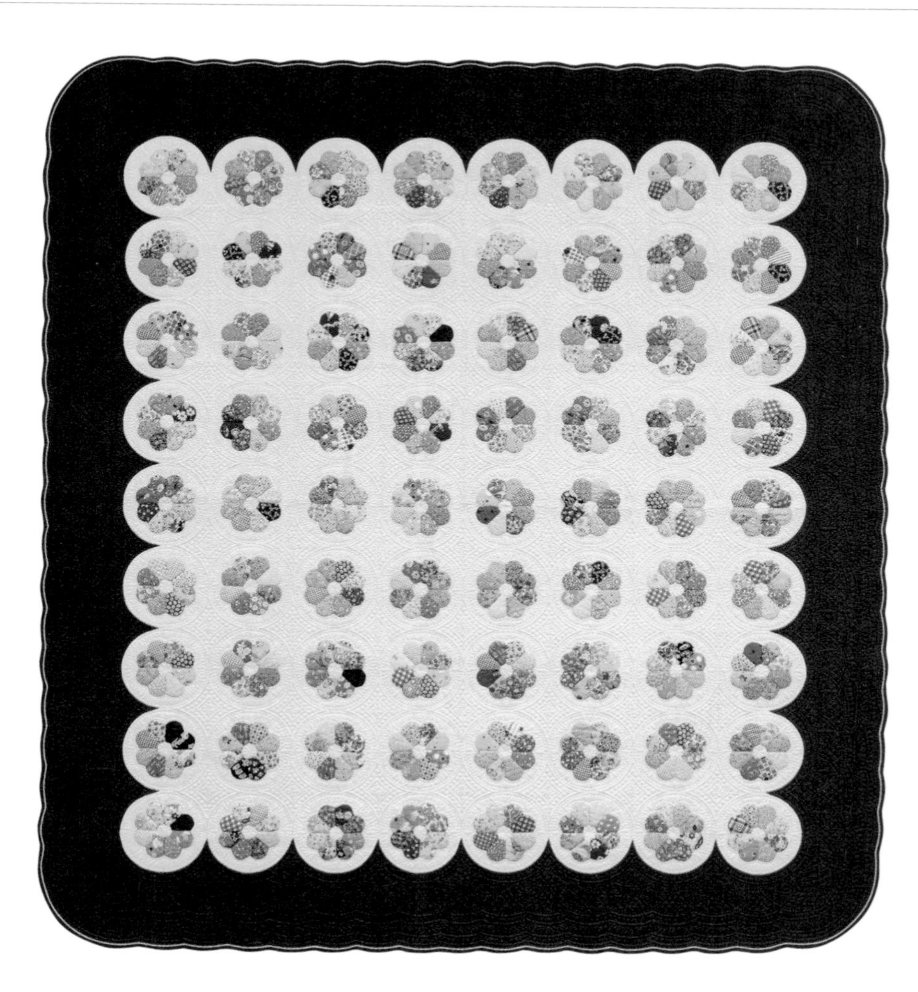

"Dresden's Dilemma," appliquéd by the late Sharon Del Pino; pieced and machine quilted by Deborah Poole; 80" x 88".

This and That

This section includes a collection of my best tips and tricks and those of friends.

MY BEST TIPS AND TRICKS

After six years as a long-arm quilter, I've tried just about every tool and technique out there. Here are some helpful hints and words of wisdom that I've picked up along the way.

Quarter-Inch Templates and Rulers

Don't think of your ¼"-thick acrylic templates and rulers as merely something you sew against. I use mine to mark quilts as well, getting double duty out of them.

Frogging

Whenever teaching a class, I tell students the most important skill you'll learn is the frog stitch. Rip it, rip it, rip it. Truthfully, sewing of any kind is only as good as the stitches you're willing to rip out and stitch again. I rip on every project at least once, most of the time much, much more often. So don't groan when you have to rip; it will make you a better quilter.

Tweezers

Nothing will perfect your frogging better than a pair of tweezers. They'll hold the offending thread while you use your seam ripper to cut the bobbin threads. They're also great for grasping and removing all the little threads after you have ripped.

Batting Pieces

I use batting squares of all sizes for a variety of uses. I have several pieces 24" wide by various lengths up to 120" to cover the belly bar and my quilt as I work. This is especially helpful when I'm working on a white or light-colored quilt, so nothing rubs off onto the quilt. I also like rectangular pieces 4" x 8" to 4" x 10". I place one on top of the quilt I'm working on to hold my seam ripper, tweezers, small scissors, and small clear templates that could otherwise easily become lost on the busy surface of the quilt top. I find that small 2" squares of batting are useful for collecting thread tails as I stitch, or for wiping excess oil from the machine.

Thread Color and Size

When stitching an allover pattern, finding a thread that works on all colors can be difficult. I've discovered that Superior's So Fine #425 (Brown Sugar, a medium brown with a bit of a red tint) thread works as a great blender for most medium to dark warm tones. So Fine #434 (Misty Blue, a dusty blue leaning toward gray) is a great blender for medium to dark cool tones. Another thing I like about So Fine thread by Superior Threads is the size. It's a 50/3 filament polyester that's lint-free and extra smooth. It disappears into the fabric and shows less thread buildup when backtracking.

Clear Vinyl

Clear tablecloth vinyl can be found at most fabric stores and is a great way to preview designs on your quilt top. Using a dry-erase marker, draw your design on the vinyl, and then place the vinyl over the quilt top. I don't draw on the vinyl while it's on top of the quilt because if I don't pay attention, I might make a stroke off the plastic and onto the quilt. Don't ask me how I know.

Open-Ended Needles

I love open-ended hand-sewing needles, called Easy Threading needles by Dritz, for tying off and burying threads. They're easy to use, and you don't have to search for your glasses to find the eye of the needle.

Dragging

If you "drag" the pick-up bar of your table on the throat of your machine, you'll gain better control. A rice bag placed on the quilt works as well. I use one of the long tubes that can be heated in the microwave to relieve sore muscles.

Crochet Hook

Sometimes I find stray threads peeking through a light background. A tiny steel crochet hook in size 14 easily and invisibly removes the offending thread. Insert the hook end into the fabric and grab the offending thread. Gently pull it up through the hole made by the hook. You may need to use a pair of tweezers to pull it completely out if you've stitched over it.

Hammer

Yes, you read that right, a hammer, although I prefer to call it a "persuader." I keep one handy that is clean and used only on quilt tops. (It also has a pink handle, so I know that my husband and son won't go near it.) Oftentimes when more than two seams meet, there's a lump at the seam intersection that can really wreak havoc, not only on your machine, but on how smooth your stitching is. I position the lump over the throat of my machine and pound it flat. You can also place a small block of wood under the area to pound on.

BEST TIPS FROM OTHER QUILTERS

I believe in giving credit where credit is due. The following tips are from fellow quilters who have suggested them to me.

Foam Core

Bethanne Nemesh of Allentown, Pennsylvania, uses ¼"-thick foam core, available at office-supply or craft stores, for making templates. She uses these low-cost alternatives not only for marking on her quilts, but against the hopping foot to guide stitching also.

Toothbrush

Linda Steller of Eugene, Oregon, uses an electric toothbrush dipped lightly in water to help close up the needle holes in fabric after frog stitching. She says this helps especially if the fabric has a firm weave, such as a batik or white-on-white print. She recommends the little battery-powered brushes rather than the full-power Sonicare model.

Glue Dots

Karen Walker of Hillsboro, Oregon, recommends using removable glue dots on the bottom of your ¼"-thick templates to keep them from slipping while you stitch.

Resources

The Calico Kitten
608-524-2697
www.thecalicokitten.com
A variety of long-arm quilting supplies, including templates and accessories

The Gadget Girls
888-844-8537
www.thegadgetgirls.com
A wonderful selection of templates

Handi Quilter
800-MY-QUILT
www.handiquilter.com
VersaTool and other templates and supplies

Innova
888-99-QUILT
www.innovalongarm.com
Long-arm quilting machines

Lakeside Quilt Company
888-361-4806
www.lovetoquilt.com
Extended base plates and a large selection of templates and stencils

Longarm University
253-854-3362
www.longarmuniversity.com
Batting, templates, notions, and tutorials

The Stencil Company
724-540-5076
www.quiltingstencils.com
A good source for ready-made stencils

Superior Threads
800-499-1777
www.superiorthreads.com
So Fine! #50 thread

Textile Time Travels
435-259-7475
gingham@frontiernet.net
Quilt appraisals, classes, trunk shows on quilt history, quilt dating, and antique quilts

Acknowledgments

First, foremost, and always, thank you to my family for supporting and appreciating my crazy "hob-jobby," for putting up with my rants and tantrums when this or that quilt didn't turn out quite as wanted, and for finally understanding I really do work on Mondays!

Many, many thanks to Kim Diehl, for giving me the opportunity to quilt your beautiful quilts, for believing my quilting had merit, for giving me the push I needed to contact Martingale, and for being an all-around great person to work with.

To Beverly Hindman, Doris Coffey, and Editha Van Orden, thank you for your superior piecework. Quilting on your masterpieces makes my job easy.

A big thank-you to the people at Martingale for giving me a chance to help others learn.

I'd like to thank my three BFFs in the quilting world, Michelle Wyman, Linda Steller, and Bethanne Nemesh. Though we are strewn to the four corners of the nation, you have been there from the start with encouragement, advice, and support. I consider you my best friends not only in quilting, but in life.

As always, I give thanks to my Father in Heaven for blessing me with this wonderful talent and giving me not only the desire to quilt, but also the need to share the things I've learned.

About the Author

Deborah Poole comes from a long line of quilters. Some of her earliest memories are of sitting in an overstuffed chair with her Grammy, cutting out hexagons from old clothes using a cardboard template and scissors while her Grammy and Great-Aunt Mary hand stitched them together. As she grew older, she was allowed to help piece and add quilting stitches to the quilts already on the frame.

The first quilt she cut and pieced completely on her own was a Golden Wedding Ring. She admits, however, that the first six-pointed stars and subsequent rings she stitched looked more like a teepee than the quilt it would become. Her Aunt Sharon, her mother's sister, reworked the block and—over the phone—talked her through how to make one correctly. At the time, Deborah was living in Tennessee, and her aunt in California.

Deborah now lives in southeastern Idaho with her husband, Jace, and claims to be an Idaho native by marriage. She is the mother of two lovely young women and a wonderful young man. She also has two terrific sons-in-law and four beautiful grandchildren, two girls and two boys.

Deborah's work can also be seen in Kim Diehl's books *Simple Graces* and *Simple Charm* as well as Kim's collaborative work with Laurie Baker, *Homestyle Quilts* (Martingale, 2010, 2012, and 2012, respectively).

Some of Deborah's awards from regional and national shows include many first and second places, plus numerous honors for Best Machine Quilting, Judge's Choice, Best of Show, and Viewer's Choice.